CROWOOD SPORTS GUIDES
RUGBY UNION

TECHNIQUE • TACTICS • TRAINING

CROWOOD SPORTS GUIDES
RUGBY UNION
TECHNIQUE • TACTICS • TRAINING

Peter Johnson

The Crowood Press

First published in 1997 by
The Crowood Press Ltd
Ramsbury, Marlborough
Wiltshire SN8 2HR

www.crowood.com

Revised edition 2009

British Library Cataloguing-in-Publication Data
A catalogue record for this book is available from the British Library.

ISBN 978 1 84797 064 0

Photographic Credits
The author and the publishers would like to thank the following clubs and
individuals for kindly providing photographs that have been included in this
book: Martin Bennett, Bristol Rugby, Filton College, Gloucester Rugby Club,
Leeds Carnegie Academy, Northampton Saints, Saracens Academy, the
South-West England Regional Academy, University of Bristol Photographic
Society, the Women's Rugby Football Union and Worcester Warriors
Academy.

Thanks are also due to Jane Haslam for taking the photographs which
appear on the following pages: 2, 6–7, 14–15, 34–35, 57, 81, 96–97 and
116–117, all of which are © Sundial Photographic.

Line drawings by Andrew Green

Designed and typeset by Focus Publishing, Sevenoaks, Kent

Printed and bound in Singapore by Craft Print International Ltd

CONTENTS

FOREWORD

This book is designed to appeal to all players, coaches and spectators of the game of Rugby Union, no matter at what level they play or coach or watch.

It highlights the major aspects of the game and breaks each component down into its technical factors. This will help players take greater responsibility for their own skill development. The benefit to coaches will be plenty of reference material to plan and construct their coaching sessions. It is also designed for the casual or knowledgeable spectator to give a greater understanding of the game and its core, unit and team skills, as well as the principles of play.

Peter's background means he has a huge bank of knowledge and understanding of the game. He was a school teacher for many years, and became involved in professional rugby when the game went open. He has been a Director of Rugby at professional club level, and a Manager of an England Regional Academy. Peter is currently internal verifier to the RFU Apprenticeship scheme.

I believe this book is a valuable addition to our literature on Rugby Union, and I have no hesitation in recommending it to anyone interested in improving as a player or coach, or to anyone who wishes to understand the game in greater depth.

Conor O'Shea
RFU Director National Academy

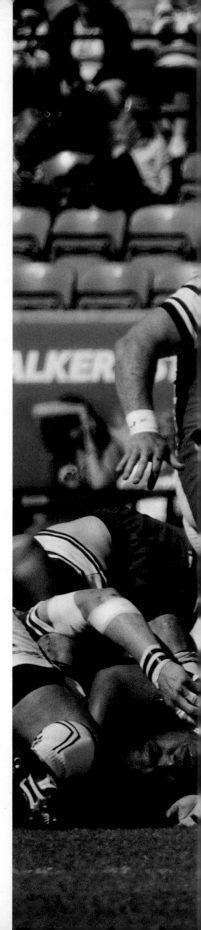

PART 1

THE GAME

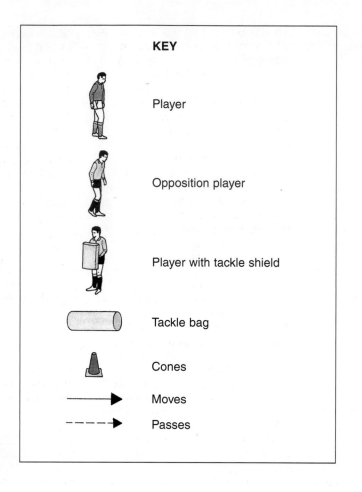

KEY

Player

Opposition player

Player with tackle shield

Tackle bag

Cones

Moves

Passes

CHAPTER 1

THE GAME OF RUGBY

The main purpose in playing rugby is to have fun. The enjoyment factor should be the main emphasis of coaches and parents, no matter what the level of rugby.

Rugby Union is a competitive, contact game, but players and coaches should never forget it is also a game which involves co-operation. Fifteen players work together to achieve victory by scoring more points than the opposition, and they also collaborate with the opposition. Two teams meet at set times to test out their skills and organization against each other within the laws of the game. Since there are so many complex situations with thirty players on the field, there is, and must be, refereeing by consensus. The players have to be self-disciplined.

The Laws and Playing of Rugby

First developed in the nineteenth century when a schoolboy at Rugby School picked up the ball and ran with it during a football game, the modern game of rugby is governed by laws that can appear complicated for the casual observer. At its simplest, however, the game is about running, handling, tackling and kicking with an oval-shaped ball, and using these skills to score points.

The game is played by fifteen players on each side, comprising eight forwards and seven threequarters, or backs. The primary role of the forwards is to provide the ball for the backs to use. Replacement players are permitted, to replace injured men, and tactical

substitutions can also be made. The number that can be replaced on each side varies according to age group and competition level. In National League Rugby in England, for example, four replacements are allowed, while up to seven replacements can be used in under-21 rugby.

For ease of identification for spectators and team-mates, each team wears different coloured shirts. In the event of teams having similar or clashing colours, the home team must change its colours.

Points are scored in a variety of ways. A try – when the ball is grounded in the opposition's in-goal area by a player from the attacking team – scores five points. Two more points can then be scored by the attacking team going on to kick a goal, spot-kicking the ball over the bar and between the upright posts. The kick can be a place or drop-kick and is taken in-field and opposite where the ball was put down in the in-goal area. The converted penalty kick has become increasingly important in the game as defences are better organized and more difficult to break down.

A further kicking option is the drop-goal, which is worth three points. In some circumstances, this can be an easier option than running with the ball to score a try.

As well as the thirty players, there are three match officials in each game. The referee keeps the score and time and applies the laws, and two touch judges decide when and where the ball goes out of play. In higher levels of rugby the touch judges also help the referee spot infringements and decide on off-side

lines, indicating these cases by holding up a flag. The referee blows a whistle to start and finish the match and for infringements of the laws. He is the sole judge of fact and has the power to send off players for repeated technical infringements or for dangerous and violent play. He can also penalize dissent from players by giving the opposition an extra 10 metres.

> ### KIT CHECK
>
> The goal posts and any barriers close to the field should be padded. Creosote mixtures to mark out the field and organic fertilizers should be avoided.

The field of play is shown in Fig 1. After the choice of ends, based on the toss of the coin, play starts with a kick-off from the halfway line in which the ball must travel at least 10 metres. If it does not travel this far, but the receiving side decides to play it, then play continues. If the kicking side plays it first then the opposition have the option for the kick to be taken again, or a scrum on the middle spot.

Eight forwards from each side participate in the scrum. They bind on to players of their own team and pack down against the opposition, meeting at the front row of three from each team. The middle player in the front row is the hooker and he has a prop forward on either side of him. They engage through the shoulders, and the head of a player

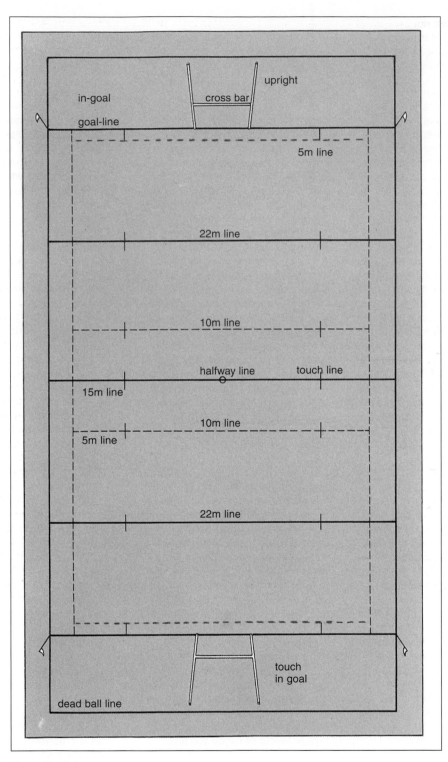

Fig 1 The playing area.

in the front row must not be next to a player of the same team. The second row generally consists of two lock forwards , who prevent the scrum being pushed back by locking out, and two flankers, who defend opposition attacks close to the scrum or support their own team attacks. At the base of the scrum is the No.8, who also has an offensive/defensive role.

Scrums are held on the 5-metre line in front of the goal-line, when the ball has been carried into the in-goal area by the attacking team, but a try has not been scored, or when the ball is carried over the goal-line by the defending side and then grounded. In each case the attacking side puts the ball into the scrum. Scrums are also awarded for a forward pass or a knock-on, which occurs when the ball strikes a player's hand or arm and is propelled forward. (If the strike was unintentional and the player recovers control of the ball before it hits the ground, however, the ball is not a knock-on.)

A scrum is formed when, after a tackle, the ball becomes dead and does not emerge into play. The laws demand that the ball must be played away from contact situations, in order to prevent the ball dying. The onus is on tackler and tackled player to roll away from the ball and make it available and neither player is allowed to play the ball again until regaining their feet. If the referee decides the ball cannot be played, and no one in particular is

responsible for the stoppage, he has to decide who puts the ball in the scrum. If the ball was held off the ground, he will decide that the ball carrier should have made it available and award the put-in to the opposition. If the ball was on the ground and the ball carrier was doing his best, he will give the ball to the carrier's side.

Another set play on the field is the 22-metre drop-out, ordered after the ball has been taken into the in-goal area by the attacking side but grounded by the defence. This drop-out can be taken anywhere along and inside the 22-metre line.

From inside his own 22-metre line a player can kick directly to touch. Outside of his own area, the ball must first bounce in the field of play before going into touch. If the ball is kicked directly into touch outside the 22-metre area, the non-offending team have a lineout opposite where the kick took place.

If the ball carrier is tackled into touch, then his side do not get the throw-in in the lineout. If a team kicks the ball into touch, that team cannot then throw the ball in. If a penalty has been awarded, it is permissible to kick directly to touch from any area in the field and get the throw-in.

When a lineout is formed, all members of the lineout must be between the 5-metre line and the 15-metre line and the ball must be thrown at least 5 metres. If the ball is knocked-on in the lineout then a scrum is formed on the 15-metre line.

Players make progress towards the opponents' line in a variety of ways. They can kick for territory or run forward with the ball and make it available for a support player when they are tackled. One of the difficult concepts for younger players to understand is how you can make progress if you can only pass backwards; not much progress would be made, if a player were to run 2 metres forwards and pass 3 metres backwards, for example. One way of explaining this is that a team makes ground by running 2 metres forwards but passing only half a metre backwards.

Another difficult law for the beginner to understand is the off-side. A player is off-side if he is in front of the ball when it has been kicked, touched or is being carried by a player from his own team who is behind him. He will be penalized only if he tries to obstruct the opposition, or moves forward, or if he makes no effort to retire when he is within 10 metres of an opponent who has retrieved a ball kicked to him. Players are off-side if they are not in the lineout and are within 10 metres of the line of touch or if they are not in the ruck and maul and the offside line at the scrum is 5m behind the hindmost foot.

A ruck occurs when the ball is on the ground and one or more players from each side make physical contact over it. A maul is formed when a ball carrier stays on his feet, the ball does not touch the ground and one or more players from each team close around him.

CHAPTER 2

SAFETY AND INJURY PREVENTION

Prevention through Fitness

Injuries are inevitable in rugby union, either self-inflicted (for example, ligament strains or muscle pulls) or as the result of an impact with another player.

Fit players who have a good aerobic and muscular endurance base and who are strong and supple are less likely to be injured than those who are unfit. Injuries caused by contact between players can be reduced if players use correct techniques when making contact with the ground, tackling, scrummaging, rucking and mauling, and if they work hard to strengthen the vulnerable neck and shoulder muscles.

Prevention through Preparation

Players can also reduce the possibility of injury with a good warm-up, which consists of a set of activities to help the body adapt from a resting state to an optimal state of readiness to play. Muscles work more efficiently and are less prone to damage when they are warm.

During a warm-up the intensity of exercise should be gradually increased so that, by the end of the warm-up, the body is working at the level at which it would have to work in a game. Warm-ups should include the kind of movements that feature in the game itself, including side-stepping, jumping and passing. This can help the player prepare mentally

as well physically. The ball should be used at most stages of a warm-up.

This is an example of a 20-minute warm-up:

*   Phase 1: slow jogging, stop, turn, at a low intensity, skipping, backwards and sideways jogging, passing a ball in 4s. Stretch calves, hamstrings, quads, hip flexors, lower back. All stretches held for 5 seconds.
*   Phase 2: faster jogging, striding out, changes of direction, high knees, heel flicks simple ball running work. Stretch calves, hamstrings, quads, adductors, hip flexors, lower back and gluteals. All stretches held for 10 seconds.
*   Phase 3: striding out followed by acceleration sprints, specific movements, grids, touch. Stretch calves, hamstrings, quads, hips, adductors, hips and gluteals. Stretches held for 15 seconds.

After the three phases, players should return to some high-intensity sprinting activity and perform specific movements such as lineouts. Threequarters will run through moves, hitting tackle shields, to ensure full readiness for the game.

The cool-down is the process by which a player helps the body to adjust gradually from exercise to rest. One of the main causes of muscular soreness and stiffness after a match is the accumulation of waste products, particularly lactic acid. Light activity can help in the removal of these waste products from the body, thus reducing the stiffness and soreness. Muscles are much more responsive to stretching after a good warm-up, training

session or match and tend to remain at their stretched length better. Stretches in the cool-down period should focus on the major muscle groups used and can be held for longer than in the warm-up.

Prevention through Protection

A properly made mouthguard is an essential piece of equipment for the rugby player. It should provide protection for the teeth, the soft tissues of the face and the gums and will also help prevent concussion. The habit of wearing a mouthguard should be encouraged among all players from a very young age. Custom-made is the only type of recommended mouthguard.

Other equipment might include shoulder pads, headgear and

KIT CHECK

*   A player must not wear shoulder pads of the harness type. The only protective clothing allowed are RFU-approved scrum caps.
*   The studs (sprigs) on a player's boots must conform to British Standard and are distinguished by the kite mark on them. A single stud at the toe is prohibited.
*   Wear gum shields which have been properly fitted by a dentist.
*   Use swimming trunks under shorts rather than 'jock straps', which can cause genital injuries.
*   Players should not wear dangerous projections such as buckles or rings.

fingerless gloves, and all these items must bear the IRB approval mark.

Boots should be comfortable and strong enough to support the ankle and Achilles tendon area, but they should not rub the bones or tendons. Studs must conform to International Rugby Board's recommendations and should be checked regularly for uneven wear. Loose studs are dangerous. A stud lost during a game can often be the cause of an ankle injury.

It is advisable to have an anti-tetanus injection before playing rugby and to have a regular booster as advised by a doctor.

Self-Discipline and Dangerous Play

Self-control is all-important in a contact sport, and retaliation must not be encouraged by emotive words and phrases and abuse of the referee by players or spectators.

Punching, kicking, tripping an opponent or stamping on him is dangerous play and will be penalized.

Late and early tackles, tackling a player above the line of the shoulders, tackling a player whilst he is in the air and charging a player without making an attempt to grab him are all deemed as dangerous tackles.

Collapsing the scrum, taking an opponent up and out of the scrum, or charging into a scrum are also illegal because they are physically dangerous.

Safe Techniques

Fig 2   Tackling.

Fig 3   Rucking.

Fig 4   Scrummaging.

PART 2

TEAM PLAY

CHAPTER 3

PRINCIPLES OF WINNING RUGBY

Win Primary Possession

Kick-offs, scrums and lineouts are different ways of restarting the game. They are called primary or set phase areas of the game. If the ball is won cleanly and delivered as the platform is moving forwards, there is a good opportunity to make use of it.

The team needs two or three lineout forwards, who can win their own ball, and an accurate thrower.

The forwards must be able to form a stable scrum to resist the opposition's attempts to push them back and disrupt their possession. Receiving and chasing kick-offs must be well organized.

Delivery of the Ball

Lineout forwards vary the timing of the release of the ball to create uncertainty in the defence. Sometimes, the ball can be caught and driven before releasing the ball. This commits the opposition back-row forwards to resisting the drive. Sometimes the ball can be deflected off the top of the jump to the scrum half, to give a very quick ball to the backs. At the scrum, Channel One ball (emerging between the legs of the left flanker and left lock) is quicker than Channel Two ball (emerging at the legs of the No.8 who is propping between the two locks). Ruck ball tends to be delivered faster than maul ball.

Score Tries by Moving the Ball

Good ball should never be wasted: players should always attack. Players must be able to pass accurately under pressure. A side needs at least three runners with pace, and it is the team's aim is to get the ball to them.

Fig 5   Mark Easter winning the lineout for Northampton Saints.

ABOVE: Fig 6   Leeds Carnegie destroy the Worcester scrum.

RIGHT: Fig 7   Score tries.

STAR TIP

Teams will be more effective if 9 and 10 are put in an armchair. Half backs know that they want a fast ball or not at all. Scrum halfs should therefore be assertive. His communication, however, must be slow and controlled so that the pack do not get panic messages and get flustered.

Richard Harding
(England)

Fig 8 Charlie Armstrong of Truro College heading for space.

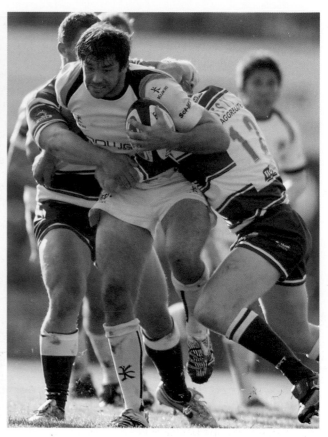

Fig 9 Pat Sanderson of Worcester Warriors drives forward.

Have a Selection of Moves

Understand the options available in different parts of the field from the various types of possession. The players must be familiar with the moves and patterns of play. The strategic and tactical decision-makers are at half-back. Does your team have these people?

Go Forwards

Gain ground. Get a ball carrier behind the defence. A team that is tackled in front of the gain-line has the advantage of the forwards being able to run ahead to ruck or maul and be dynamic. The opposition is on its heels, whilst the attacking side is on its toes.

Support the Ball Carrier

The ball carrier should have immediate help, if required, and passing options on either side of him. The ball carrier must not get isolated. If support is not close, he should go looking for it. Support players require an understanding of body language – knowing whether the ball carrier will plant the ball on the ground or pass it – which will be learned in practice.

The players must be physically fit to be good at support play, but getting immediate support also demands formal communication so that the players know in which area or channel of the field the ball is to be used and the breakdown planned. The wider the ball is played from the forwards, the fewer can get to the breakdown, and the harder it is to retain the ball. The further behind the gain-line the breakdown occurs, the more difficult it is to retain the ball; the further in front, the better.

Disorganize the Defence

A team needs players who can take the ball into contact to disrupt the defence, and players who are able to react to the disorganized defence.

Retain Possession

Ball retention at contact is the key to success. Much depends on player attitude, skills and tactics. The ball carrier must be aware of his responsibility which ends only when he makes the ball available to another player. Much depends on his work rate between the point at which he is tackled and when he hits the ground.

The ball carrier needs to be able to recognize high-risk situations. He should take care not to take the ball too far, put effort into retaining possession, and be calm on the ball.

A team's options are to pass, run or kick. Which is best for your team, if you wish to succeed in ball retention?

Head for Space

Space always exists on the pitch, but it gets moved around. There is space between defenders, on the edges of a group of defenders, behind and in front of defenders. Move quickly into the space in front of defenders. To turn defences, kick the ball into the space behind defenders.

Recognize the shape of the game: if the defence is spread, penetrate by attacking the space between defenders; if the defence is concentrated, outflank it.

The ball carrier bases his decisions on the distribution of the defenders. Split fields, as in the case of a midfield scrum, give the attacking side more options

and the defence is spread over a wider area.

Kick Only When Necessary

The team should have a kicking strategy. For example, long tactical kicking down the tram-lines forces the opposition to find touch. It can win distance, and your side can recover the ball by gaining the throw at the resultant lineout.

It is important to follow all kicks in organized depth to pressurize the opposition. Tackle them deep in their own territory or force a mistake. Tactical kickers at fly half and full back are needed.

Continuity is the Key

Recycle the ball quickly in contact situations. Sustain the attack. The speed of delivery of the ball in the tackle to the next wave of attackers depends on the determination of the ball carrier to get the ball back in a controlled fashion and the speed of the support players to the breakdown.

Communication

There should be lineout signals, and coded calls for moves in the threequarters. The back row should be told where the threequarters are going to strike so they can make their way to the estimated collision point. Threequarters should be told where the ball is to be thrown in the lineout. The back row should tell the threequarters if they are doing a back-row move. The fly half should override back-row moves if there is a clash. If kicking, the chasers must be told. In defence, there should be communication between players so no one is in doubt about who is going to tackle which opposing player.

Fig 10   Mark Hopley (Northampton Saints), the ball carrier, being closely supported by Ben Lewitt.

Fig 11   Carlos Spencer makes a tactical kick into space.

Kick Goals

Goal-kickers win matches. Is there a goal-kicker in the team?

Pressurize the Opposition Ball

Go forward to defend. Defend your own 22-metre area as if it were your goal-line. A tackle should be a means of winning back the ball. All players must be capable of making offensive tackles.

Each player should understand the defensive organization and his role in it. Does the team have the ability to spread defenders across the field who are able to defend their own channels?

Cover Back as a Scramble Defence

If the ball has been kicked behind your own defence, players must get back quickly between the ball and their own goal-line.

Play with Confidence

Do the players have the necessary mental skills? Are the players patient or do they panic? Do they have confidence in the game plan and their own ability to cope with it? Are they positive? Do they recognize the difference between a risk and a gamble? Do the players support each other's mistakes and encourage each other?

Self-Discipline

Do the players know the laws? Can they keep their mouths shut or do they upset the referee? Do they retaliate if provoked?

Change Gear

Do the players change gear at breakdowns? Do they lift their game at key times and positions? Do they turn 50/50 ball into 60/40 ball?

CHAPTER 4

STRATEGY AND TACTICS

Preparation

Team preparation is the responsibility of the coach and poor preparation will lead to a poor performance. For the coach, the most exciting part of rugby is putting together a range of options, patterns of play and contingency game plans that are suitable to the individual and unit skills of his team, in order to produce a winning combination.

In order to achieve success, the coach has to make every player in his team aware of his positional role, its requirements, why he personally has been selected, his potential contribution to the team, his own limitations and what the other players of his team are capable of doing.

Strategy

Strategy dictates the pattern that the players are trying to execute. It is based upon an analysis of the strengths and weaknesses of the team. A team's style of play depends on the individual and collective skills of the players and units. The first decision – which channel to strike in – is taken at first phase. Other decisions involve how to recycle the ball (ruck or maul), how to play after a breakdown (again, which channel to strike in) and where and when to kick.

A game plan is part of the strategic plan. It is designed for a specific game, when the strengths and weaknesses of the opposition have been analysed.

Tactics

Tactics are the various options available to the team in carrying out the strategy. If the strategic aim is to strike wide, the different ways of getting the ball wide are the tactics; for example, they may choose a decoy move close to the forwards, to hold up opponents and buy some time and space for the players wide out, or they may decide to move the ball wide with long, miss-out passes rather than moving the ball through every pair of hands in the threequarter line. However, the range of tactics is limited by the range of the individual skills available. Long passes are not feasible, for example, if the players involved do not have the necessary handling skills.

In the diagram and explanation below are a range of suggested tactical options in various parts of the field. What is chosen depends on the team strategy. If the forwards are good in the set pieces and the threequarters are slow and unreliable handlers, why not choose the kicking options and attempt to play from set piece to set piece?

Inside your own 22-metre area (Zone 1), the ball must be controlled. Everyone must concentrate. Every metre matters and must be defended. The greatest difficulty is between the 22-metre lines (Zones 2, 3, 4). Here, patterns of play have to be developed to move the ball closer to the opposition goal-line. It is a developmental or transitional area as a team gathers for the last strike that will lead to the score. A metre does not matter in this area as much as it does inside the 22-metre areas. A great deal of effort is expended in this area for little return. Inside the opposition 22 metres (Zone 5), pressure is applied. The team must be patient, try out their ploys, and be aware that every metre matters.

STAR TIP

We must have the ability to mix it up. Whether we run the ball, play field position or utilize fitness and flair with our handling and kicking, the most important point is that we must do it well. It's not so much what we do, but how close we come to excellence in execution.

Bob Dwyer
(Australia, National Coach)
(International Rugby Review, 1995)

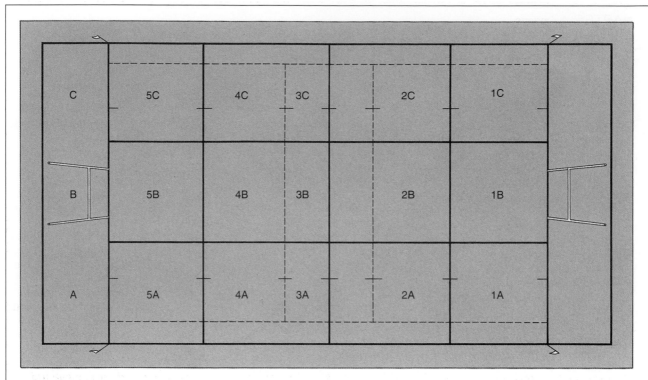

Fig 12   Tactical options.

Tactics: Options in Areas of the Field

Own 22m zone; positions 1A, 1B and 1C; find touch.

Area	Options
1A	1. Outside half or full back kick to left touch-line. 2. Get ball to outside centre who kicks to right touch-line. 3. Move the ball wide to the right wing.
1B	1. Scrum. See where they have their 11, 14 and 15. Kick to touch. Outside half goes right and kicks to right touch-line or outside half stands left, full back stands right and receives pass from scrum half to kick right or outside half stands right, passes to full back or right centre to find touch. 2. Backs move going right.
1C	1. Lineout: left-footed kicker needed at outside half to kick to right touch-line; pass ball to left-footed kicker at outside centre and kick to left touch-line. 2. Scrum: slight possibility of 9, 14 break right; kick to right touch by outside half or full back standing behind or to right of scrum.

Own 22m to own 10m line; positions 2A, 2B and 2C; control, drive and kick; chasers.

Area	Options
2A	1. Scrum: high ball to 3A or 3B. Scrum half or outside half kicks to 3A with left wing and inside centre chasing. 2. Lineout: catch, drive, box kick to 3A from scrum half or long kick along tramlines to 4A by outside half. Chase the kicks. Backs move?

Area	Options
2B	1. Back row goes right.
	2. Split field, backs move going to the right.
	3. Diagonal kick to 3C,4C.
2C	1. Scrum: box kick to 4C.
	2. Scrum: possibility of 9 and 14 break.
	3. Lineout: catch, drive, kick along tramlines by outside half to 4C, 5C.

Between the 10m lines: positions 3A, 3B and 3C; control, drive and kick or run.

Area	Options
3A	1. Scrum: back row infield, backs attack narrow side after breakdown or Backs ball.
	2. Outside half box kicks to 4A with inside centre and left wing chasing or high bomb to 4B with both centres chasing.
	3. Lineout: backs move hitting edge of midfield or committing midfield; forward stand off from second phase.
	4. Lineout: catch, drive, 6 and 7 take on.
3B	1. Backs move going right.
	2. Back row going right.
	3. Kick to 5A or 5C
3C	1. Scrum: box kick to 4C.
	2. Backs move going left.
	3. Scrum: back row move to right; second phase forward standing off.
	4. Scrum: back row go left and backs go right at the breakdown.

Opponents' 10m to 22m zone; positions 4A, 4B and 4C. Preparation: running rugby: strike narrow, move wide.

Area	Options
4A	1. Scrum: box kick by outside half or scrum half to 5A or bomb by outside half to 5B with both centres chasing.
	2. Two-man lineout. Drop-goal.
4B	1. Backs move going right.
	2. Back row going right.
4C	1. Scrum: box kick to 5C.
	2. Backs move going left.
	3. Scrum: back row move to right; second phase forward standing off.
	4. Scrum: back row go left and backs go right at the breakdown.

Opponents' 22m zone; positions 5A, 5B and 5C; score.

Area	Options
5A	1. Lineout: peel.
	2. Scrum: back row.
	3. Backs ball.
5B	1. Drop-goal.
	2. Back row.
	3. Backs move going right.
5C	1. Lineout: peel.
	2. Scrum: back row.
	3. Backs ball.

Team Patterns

When the breakdown occurs, winning the ball in one of the three channels (A, B and C), and using it in different channels means that the players involved in the breakdown will differ in personnel and numbers. If the ball is won in A and the breakdown occurs in C; only a limited number of forwards will be involved in support, therefore, the threequarters should support each other. However, if the ball is won in Channel C and used in C, most of the forwards should be in support.

Here are some examples of sequences off lineouts.

Example 1

The ball is thrown to the tail of the lineout. The scrum half passes to the inside centre who takes it into contact. The non-jumping and lifting pod of forwards hit the first ruck.

The scrum half passes to 10, and receives a return pass. The outside centre runs back towards 9 to hold the drift defence and 9 passes behind 13 to the blind-side wing with full back and open-side wing in support.

Example 2

The ball is thrown to the tail. The scrum half passes to the inside centre who goes into contact. The same pod of forwards win the first ruck.

The scrum half pops the ball to a forward runner from the jumping and lifting pod to set up the second ruck. 10 and 15 go blind with blind-side wing.

Example 3

The ball is thrown to the tail of the lineout; scrum half passes to fly half who passes to inside centre. 12 dummy scissors with 13, and passes to 8. The first ruck is set up.

Forwards not going to first ruck carry on normal line as runners. 9 to 10 running back to the blind-side with the open-side wing and 15.

10 passes to OSW. 2 runs back towards OSW to hold drift defence. OSW passes to 15 with BSW in support.

More Sequences

1. Scrum left (Zone 5A). No.8 picks up, going right. He is tackled by the opposition open-side flanker. The supporting blind-side flanker and left lock clear out the opposition who are converging over the ball, and the scrum half gives a soft pass to the loose head prop also going right and running fast and close to the breakdown. He gets tackled (Zone 5B) and the forwards clear out the opposition for the scrum half to give the ball to the threequarters either going open (to score from 5C) or switching back in the direction of the original scrum (5A).

2. Receiving kick-off (Zone 2C). Blind-side flanker or wing receive a pass going down the narrow side. When tackled, a ruck is formed (Zone 3C) and the ball is passed to the threequarters who carry out a midfield move (3B). Another ruck is formed and the ball is passed wide to score from Channel A.

3. Lineout in Zone 5A. A back peel is stopped and a ruck follows in 5B. This is followed by a midfield move and another ruck in 5B. The ball is switched back to Channel A to score.

CHAPTER 5

SELECTING THE TEAM

Selection, Strategy and Tactics

Strategy and tactics are associated with selection. Do you select the best players and then determine your strategy? Alternatively, do you decide on strategy first and then go looking for the players who are best suited to carrying out the plan? Do you select several outstanding players, choose a strategy based on their talents and then fill in the other positions with players who can complement their skills? The decision depends on the coach's preference and the situation.

Selection Considerations

Are the positional requirements compatible with the player's skills? For example, should you pick a No.8 as an open-side flanker to give you extra height at the back of the lineout, even if he cannot defend properly or get to the breakdown quickly enough?

Do the players in the sub-units complement each other? Does the back row have a destroyer and a creator? How well do they work off each other? Do the inside and outside centres' talents create a balanced partnership? Are there two locks who can play at No.2 and No. 4 in the lineout?

The Need for a Kicker

Should a full back who is poor under the high ball be moved to the wing to find him a place in the team because he is an outstanding goal-kicker?

The Need for a Captain

The leader may not be the best player in his position, but he is worth a place in the team because of his personality and astute decision-making. Where can a place be found for him? Which positions lend themselves to captaincy?

Effective Selection

Good coaches need to have good management skills, understand the game and be good selectors. A simple system of recording what happened and why is useful and filming matches will help. Relying on memory is notoriously inefficient.

They will utilize available playing resources and be able to justify their decisions. After picking the team and replacements, they consider cover for each position for last-minute eventualities.

A good coach will make sure that the players are aware of their positional roles.

Dropping Players

Give due consideration to the dropping of players from the team. A good

---

player does not become a bad player overnight because of one poor performance. Give warning to players if their place in the team is being reviewed as a result of a number of poor games.

A player who is dropped is entitled to an explanation and advice on what to do to get reinstated. The player should be told by the coach as soon as possible. To avoid embarrassment and save his feelings, he should be told in private before the team is announced.

Positional Requirements

Each player has specialist positional skills. In general play, however, every player should be able to run, catch, pass, tackle and retain the ball on contact. All the basic skills should be taught to young players. It would be wrong to categorize children too early in their rugby careers. Children develop at different rates and to grade a young player as a prop forward, and then deny him access to the skills that are taught to threequarters is doing him a disservice. The youngster may eventually become agile and fast and a perfect specimen for a wing threequarter. Below, in summary, are the requirements of each position.

Full Back (15)

The full back is the last line of defence. He has to tackle well off either shoulder, be secure under the high ball, and be able to kick accurately off both feet. Due to his position, he has a panoramic vision

---

> **STAR TIP**
>
> It is easy to be a reasonably good coach, but far harder to be a good selector. It is a gift to be able to pick the right player at the right time in the right team.
>
> Kitch Christie
> (South Africa, National Coach)
> (International Rugby Review, 1995)

of the game, especially from phase ball and he is required to anticipate, scan, act and communicate on what he sees. He should organize the attack as well as the defence. The full back is a key attacking player from set and broken play. He must be confident and adventurous. He enters the threequarter line at various places and at different angles. With a positive attitude towards launching counter-attacks and an ability to work with his wings both in defence as well as attack, a full back can be one of the most influential players on the field, despite his remoteness from the rest of his team. Goal-kicking and restarts are a plus.

Wing (11 and 14)

He should be able to play either left or right side. Sustained and explosive speed, acceleration and evasive running skills are crucial. He needs the ability to beat opponents off either foot and stay up in the tackle when required.

In attack, the wing must be aware of the touch-line. If driven into touch, he loses possession of the ball because the resulting lineout throw will be given to the opposition. If the space is not available on the outside of a defender, the wing must be able to come inside.

He should have an awareness of blind-side options and entry into the line (inside or outside the fly half) from blind-side as an attacking or decoy option. Wings should have a hunger for involvement in the game and a high work rate. Too many wings fail to show initiative off the ball and fail to create opportunities and make play because they stay on their wing.

The wing should chase and pressure opposition whenever possible, support the full back and work in tandem on counter-attack and defence.

Outside Centre (13)

The outside centre needs explosive speed and power, and the ability to step off either foot and beat a defender on the inside and outside. Kicking skills are important, and he should be especially good at chip and grubber kicks in behind opposition backs and at the long kick out of defence.

He is a key decision-maker, especially in defence and when attacking from broken play, so he needs the ability to read the game with good tactical sense. He must have a high work rate because he is a key support player at the tackle, in following kicks and in cover defence.

His ability to pass quickly and accurately off either hand should not be under-estimated. He must also be able to carry the ball two-handed for continuity and distribution and stay up in the tackle to offload at or through the tackle. He must commit defenders with running lines, and promote support players, inside and out.

Inside Centre (12)

The inside centre is the linch-pin for much of the backline attack and defence. He is a key decision-maker and communicator especially in defence and when on attack from broken play. He must have the ability to read situations and use appropriate tactics.

Distribution skills under pressure are essential. After passing, the player offers support and also tries to anticipate where he can get involved again.

Kicking is a necessary skill for this

Fig 13   Centre Claire Allen charging through the French defence.

position because, if the fly half wants the ball kicked diagonally (say, from Channel A to Channel C), it is better done from the inside-centre position. He must be able to punt for clearance (preferably on the alternate foot from 10 or 13), and have a range of kick options to get ball in behind the position (grubber, chip and long kicks).

The inside centre must be physically strong because he has to tackle opponents head on. He often takes the ball into contact areas and must be able to retain possession. He must commit the defence with good running lines and be strong enough to stay up in the tackle.

Fly Half (10)

Much of the team's tactics revolve around the fly half. It is vital that he has good tactical sense with the ability to read the game and change tactics when necessary. His ball skills, decisiveness, calmness, elusive running and accurate kicking make him one of the most influential players on the field

He takes restarts, finds touch and kicks the bomb for designated players to chase and recover the ball; he sets lines of attack and defence; he is quickly in position from phase play and has good positional awareness from set phase. He will vary his position and the point of attack.

Fig 14 James Phillips (Bristol Rugby No.8) shows defensive qualities.

Scrum Half (9)

The scrum half gets the ball more often than any other player on the field. He is the link between backs and forwards. He needs speed to breakdowns and he must have vision. He must be able to clear ball quickly and accurately off either hand from the ground or chest. If there is space, particularly on the blind-side, his running must be explosive. His other option is to kick accurately to relieve pressure and create attacking options (box kick).

He must have organizational and communication skills and boss the forwards in attacking and defensive situations.

In defence he must be a strong and aggressive tackler, he has to tackle forwards.

He will have a high work rate, and be energetic and a real livewire.

No.8

He is a key attacking option and must have the strength and speed to breach the gain-line from scrum and

> **STAR TIP**
>
> Good hands are vital if you are one of the forwards who comes into contact with the ball regularly. I always take part in the handling drills at the club with the backs.
> Dean Richards
> *(England)*
> *(Rugby World, 1995)*

other phases, and must also be able to go wide to support. He tends to be chosen for his strong, aggressive driving and close-quarter tackling round the fringes of secondary phases. A No.8 provides a lineout option either as an effective lifter or jumper.

The No.8 tends to be the second player to the breakdown (after the open-side flanker) and must provide immediate support. His decision-making is crucial here: whether to step over the ball and protect it, pick it up and run on, or pick it up and pass it.

> **STAR TIP**
>
> The scrum half must clear the ball as quickly as possible. I only use the dive pass when I'm under pressure. I prefer the standing pass because with the dive pass you are out of action for a couple of seconds.
> Joost van der Westhuizen
> *(South Africa)*
> *(SA Rugby, 1995)*

Fig 15   *Gavin Quinnell, at 2.01m and 138kg, has the versatility to play at No.8, flanker or lock.*

In defence from the lineout, the No.8 first considers the scrum half breaking around the tail, and then supports the flanker to tackle the fly half, if he steps inside the flanker. At defending scrums, the No.8 takes the second player around.

His understanding of moves and options makes him a key player and communication link. His skills are excellent ball control, pick-up and distribution, his defensive involvement, organization and understanding, and his strong hunger to get to ball.

Open-Side Flanker (7)

This player is a non-stop hunter who never loses sight of the ball! In attack, No.7's role is to get to the breakdown first and secure the loose ball, and to be the link man to maintain the momentum of an attack. Anticipation is vital to identify the correct running lines to get to the breakdown. An open-side flanker has to be quick and have a high aerobic capacity in order to keep up with the non-stop action demanded by his position. He plays a vital role in the process of retaining and improving continuity of attack. He tends to be an intuitive rather than a re-active player

The role of the open-side flanker in defence is to destroy. He must exert pressure on the fly half from scrums and lineouts and must try to avoid being sucked into any forward play from a lineout. He must have the ability to secure ball on the ground and present it.

Blind-Side Flanker (6)

This flanker needs pace, power and strength to provide impetus at breakdowns. He has to stop the opposition forwards crossing the gain-line. He takes the first player coming around the blind side of the scrum and must be a strong, aggressive tackler.

In scrums, he adds as much weight as possible to help his props. In attack, he will often be used in back row moves to cross the gain-line. Due to his size, he will tend to be a lineout option, whether as jumper, lifter or driver.

The blind-side flanker will be one of the first players to the breakdown, usually second or third, and has to create and assist the continuity of attacks.

Locks (4 and 5)

Being the shorter of the two locks, No.4 generally jumps at No.2 in the lineout. No.5 is normally the bigger of the two locks and he jumps at No.4 in the lineout. He will usually pack down on the right side of the scrum and will use his bulk to help prevent the natural wheel of the scrum. Because of their role in the restarts (chasing and receiving) as well as in lineouts, the locks require great aerial skills.

Both locks need to have scrum power and know how to manipulate the scrum.

A lock should have the mobility to support phase ball and be an effective second-wave attacker or decoy.

Props (1 and 3)

The laws of the game have depowered the scrum at junior level, but scrummaging is still important at senior level. The tight-head prop (3) has to lock his own scrum and stop it going backwards. On the opposition ball, he has to disrupt them as far as possible. He has to take a lot more weight than the loose-head prop because of the mechanics of the scrum, and he tends to be the bigger of the two props. The major role of the loose-head prop (1) is to support his hooker in the scrums. On the opposition's ball he is trying to be as disruptive as possible. Both need to understand how to manipulate the scrum, and to be able to do it, whichever side is putting in the ball.

In the lineout and the restart

Fig 16   Prop Nick Wood (Gloucester) attempts the charge down.

receipt, the props have to work in tandem to lift the jumper. This requires agility and timing. Both need strength and physical presence especially in the upper body for lift support and scrum.

They must understand their role in defence around the phase areas and be key communicators at these defensive phases. When caught in the backs at defensive situations they should shuffle in.

In attacking phases, they should get into key second-wave attack positions with depth, and pose a threat either as ball carrier or decoy.

Hooker (2)

The hooker's most important job is to throw in the ball accurately at the lineout. In the scrum, he has to strike the ball back, and control the scrum with his props.

He will command the defence at the front of the lineout and when left on short side.

He will be a fourth loose forward in general play, making bonus tackles or getting into effective second-wave positions as attacker and decoy.

CHAPTER 6
BUILDING THE TEAM

Team Management

Professional clubs will have a coaching structure consisting of a head coach (either a forwards or backs specialist) and assistant coach, who covers the specialist area not covered by the head coach. There may be other coaches who specialize in areas such as defence or kicking. The support staff could include an operations director (or team manager), a performance analyst who uses a range of computer software to analyse the opposition and his own team, a strength and conditioning coach, and even a doctor, physiotherapist and massage therapist.

Outside the professional game, however, the numbers involved in team management, and the roles they adopt, will depend on the circumstances. Generally, a team will be managed by a team coach and his assistant, along with a manager and a team captain.

Team Coach

The team coach is responsible for the whole squad of players. He must work out a coaching philosophy for the whole club or school and team of coaches. He should create a coaching structure and define the roles of each coach.

Working together, the coaches and captain, must plan the season to target matches and establish goals, objectives and priorities. A playing style, tactics and team organization will be discussed. Rules on selection will be made. Itineraries for match days, game plans for specific matches, match preparation and match analysis are the responsibilities of the coach. Methods of individual and team feedback (meetings, video and statistics) will need to be considered. In a club, player development and recruitment will be a major concern as weaknesses in the team are highlighted. The development of the players will need monitoring and a medical strategy should be created to cope with injuries. Training objectives will relate to specific individual, unit and team skills.

Team Manager

A team manager should attend selection meetings, training, rugby committees and matches. He is responsible for informing the players about selection and ensuring that they are all familiar with the itinerary. He is a point of contact about problems, availability, injury and expenses.

Captain

How is the captain selected? Is he elected by players or appointed by the coach?

His functions are to work with the coach in planning the season,

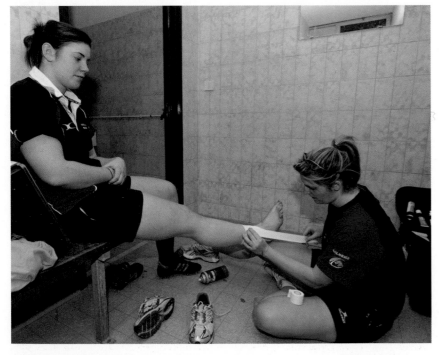

Fig 17 A physiotherapist within the team management structure is extremely important in making sure players are physically capable of taking to the field.

Fig 18   A cohesive Oaklands College team.

strategy, tactics, game plans, training objectives, briefing the players, evaluating the team performance, motivating the players, organizing training and match itineraries, and setting an example. He should have a major input in selection, lead the warm-up on match days and be good at motivating players. He has to be able to get on with the referee and be able to make decisions on the field.

Team Spirit

Players get satisfaction from a good team performance and team spirit increases motivation. Motivation is a desire to reach a specific target, and is further enhanced if those targets are reached because players are encouraged by success. Realistic and attainable goals should be set. Many coaches make the mistake of setting an outcome goal for every match, usually victory. However, there are too many variables affecting the outcome: the referee's interpretation of the laws, the weather, the opposition. It is better instead to set performance goals (75 per cent of all tackles must be effective, for example) and take statistics to see if those goals are achieved. Performance targets places the emphasis on effort and performance rather than on outcomes. If the team concentrates on the way it plays, victory could well follow. If defeated, however, a team may still get positive feedback from the tackle statistics. Alternatively, it may have identified a problem on which it can work.

A system of feedback and rewards recognizes the value of individual and unit contributions to success. Personal performances should be valued even when losing. It is important to morale to highlight the areas of success even in defeat.

Team standards that lead to better performances can be developed by coaches, in consultation, arriving at a set of do's and don'ts ('Habits') and practice rules, such as being punctual for training. Pre-season syndicate work to discuss playing strategy and seasonal goals, and pre-match meetings to discuss the opposition, and how to play them, make the players feel involved in the decision-making processes. As a result, they will feel more responsible for seeing a successful completion of the goals. Greater commitment and effort will be given.

The open exchange of ideas through team meetings also prevents poor decisions going unchallenged and avoids or resolves conflicts and resentments. However, autocratic coaches tend to frustrate and demoralize those players who are thinkers and want responsibility. They rarely give credit where it is due, normally claiming the credit for success for themselves and blaming others for failure.

Selection can also help. The fewer changes made to a team, the more stable and cohesive it will become. Players will be able to predict what certain players will do in certain situations. Accurate anticipation produces correct reactions.

Team spirit can also be encouraged by socializing together, and by developing feelings of a collective identity and a team culture, through customs, songs, behaviours, team uniforms and privileges.

Communication

Pre-Match Talks

What should be the content of the pre-match talk and how should it be conducted? The focus should be on the coming event, and not on previous performances. Little time should be spent on discussing the opposition. If the players are focused on how to stop the opposition rather than on their own playing strategy, they will become too anxious about the opposition and forget to play their own game.

The coach must clarify what is expected of each player. There is a stable, positional effort that each player must make every match. Each fulfils the responsibility of his own position. There is also an optional effort that players can make to show the crowd they are trying hard and want to win – for example, chasing the ball even when it is pointless because it is rolling over the line, or tackling when they do not often get involved. The coach could ask individual players what they could do to show everyone that they are trying extra hard.

The units should have a chance to discuss how they are going to play it and iron out any problems which have come up in training or discuss organization with new players. The coach could discuss match goals. What do the backs expect from the forwards? The backs could discuss and come up with three expectations that they will communicate to the forwards when the team gets together. Similarly, what do the forwards expect from the backs?

Half-Time Talks

Half-time talks are important to highlight areas that are of concern and the way to play the second half. The captain or coach should keep his message short and concise. He should give advice to one or two individuals about the way they can improve their performance, a message to the forwards as a unit, a message to the backs as a unit, and make one or two tactical points.

Feedback

Individual Performance

Individual feedback to the players about their performance can be achieved by a selector (or injured player) observing and reporting back to the player. If available, a video would be useful to concentrate on individuals for twenty-minute spells.

Assessments are used as feedback for the players to help them improve. They are useful also to coaches and selectors.

The best time to feed the information to the player is soon after the match. If the results are disappointing, it may be worthwhile waiting until everyone is in a more stable emotional mood and more receptive to advice. Good assessments are factual. They should interpret the facts and be informative. Constructive guidance can then be given.

There are several ways of assessing players. If everything a player does in a match is recorded, there can be too much information for a player to absorb. It is better to collect statistics on one or two chosen aspects of an individual's play, for example, his tackling or ball-retention skills. One quick route involves asking the player to assess his own strengths and weaknesses, and to discuss with the coach the area of his game on which he needs to work.

Team Performance

Analysis of team performances can fall into several categories. Possession counts at the scrum, lineout and restarts, and ruck and maul and tackle counts are all statistics that need careful interpretation. The team can also look at the statistics in relation to areas of the field: where lineouts and scrum were held and where play broke down. The ways in which the ball was used and the success rate are most interesting for the players and the coach.

Team Practices

Decision-Making

Five forwards and four backs against five forwards and two backs. No score on first phase (start from lineouts or scrums); run first-phase ball into contact and play from there.

Team Patterns – Unopposed

If they are unopposed, the forwards tend to overshoot the rucks. This is unrealistic and then they are too far in front to support their backs from second phase. Their running lines are messed up. To prevent this, make the ball carrier put down the ball and turn to provide some resistance.

Three forwards start on the 15-metre line where it meets their own 22-metre line. The threequarters start in the same place on the opposite side of the field. On the command, the threequarters run to their own goal-line, do 5 press-ups and run into position as the attacking backs. The forwards, meanwhile, run across the field to the position the backs previously occupied. The coach gives them the ball in a variety of ways. They progress down the field inter-passing until the coach shouts 'Tackle'. The forwards set up a maul or ruck and distribute to the threequarters who are now in position. Rules: 80 per cent effort; every short blast of the whistle, the ball carrier to simulate a tackle and either ruck or maul; no mistakes or sloppy play; on a long blast of the whistle, everyone is to run back to another ball thrown into play by the coach.

From each ball there should be a variation from the backs. Backs are not to drift across and run away from forwards. Backs should regard themselves as loose forwards as well. Open-side flanker link with breakdown and next forward.

Conditioned Opposed

Two teams at slow pace. The opposition are not to interfere with ball. The coach has a second ball.

When he shouts 'Change', everyone repositions on the other ball, and the first ball is returned to the coach. He can use this when things go wrong and movement is stopped. Dynamic rugby is to be played, keeping the ball alive as long as possible. Quick ball, play wide. When coach shouts 'Penetrate', they go forwards and penetrate with backs or forwards. Give to backs and support. Give to forwards when backs cannot go for gaps because they are covered. If you cannot go on, then give your support. Give the ball before contact. Penetrate and keep going until the defence is narrow and the players on the edges have been sucked in. Now play it wide. If defence is narrow, spread the ball wide. If the defence is wide, penetrate. Look for space and numbers. Sometimes give to the team going backwards.

Fully Opposed

Team against team. Five lives to score. Start in different field positions inside the opposition 22-metre line. Intense play with rest in between, with a quick discussion about the plays and outcomes.

PART 3
CORE SKILLS

CHAPTER 7
EVASION

Individual Evasive Skills

The evasive skills of the back-row players and scrum half are invaluable, if they can make the half-break by getting just behind the immediate defender and passing to a close support runner.

Midfield players who are able to make an inside break by a side-step or dummy, or can master acceleration and change of direction inside the defender can be the focal point for the back row on a first-phase attack. The outside centre, wings and full back who can take the outside gap through a swerve or change of pace will be a source of fear to the opposition.

There are common points in the preliminaries to beating defenders whether by a swerve, side-step or change of pace. Run straight at the defender and conceal your speed by slowing down or controlling your running. Be well balanced. Do not get too close to the defender before starting your evasive actions.

The Swerve

Aim for the defender's inside shoulder and, in plenty of time, swing away with a long stride across the body, leaning away from the defender with your weight on the far leg. Control the pace, straighten up by transferring the weight to the inside leg, and accelerate away.

The Side-Step

Shorten the strides and drive off the inside leg at right-angles. Put the weight on the driving leg, compressing the leg at the knee like a coiled spring, and drive off with a wide step.

The Dummy

The ball carrier should look at the player for whom the pass is intended. The arms swing out as if to pass, but the ball back is brought back to the chest. The weight will be on the inside foot and the outside foot steps across the body to set off in the opposite direction.

Variation of Pace

Run below top speed then accelerate as the tackler is about to launch himself. Lengthening and shortening the stride (the goose-step) makes the tackler hesitate and puts him off balance.

Fend Off

This is usually done when the tackler is approaching from an angle. The arm is bent and then straightened as the hand pushes off the tackler's body (his head or shoulders).

Breaking the Tackle

Turn hip and side into the tackler to bounce him off, going from a low body position to high. One shoulder tends to lead. Use forearm and shoulder to fend off.

Fig 19   Mike Rawlings (Truro College) uses footwork to force the defender to make an arm tackle.

Beating Defenders

Fig 20   Defender passes and runs around white cone to defend.

Fig 21   Attacker to run around his cone.

Fig 22   He holds up the defender bringing his leg across his body and shifting his weight to execute a swerve.

Fig 23   He holds up the defender by coming in field and running below full speed.

Fig 24   He accelerates away bringing his leg across his body and shifting his weight to execute a swerve.

Fig 25   He straightens up by leaning towards the tackler ready to hand him off and moving his legs and hips away.

The Side-Step

Fig 26 *The ball carrier accelerates through the white cones and tries to score on a line to his right. The defender runs through his gate to tackle him.*

Fig 27 *The ball carrier has a low body position and holds the ball in two hands ready to make a pass. He drives off left foot and accelerates away in the opposite direction.*

Evasive Running Exercises

Change of Pace and Direction

The players should jog 3m and sprint 3m; then jog 3m, sprint 2m left or right and 1m straight; then jog 3m, sprint 3m left or right.

Side-Step

In pairs, A standing opposite B. The ball is on the ground 3 paces in front of B. A sprints, picks up, changes direction left or right and adds pace to get past B.

Swerve or Side-Step

Form four groups, one in each corner of a 15 × 15m grid (Fig 28). Poles or traffic cones act as obstacles. Group A players run through 3 gates and exchange a ball with Group B. Group C do the same with Group D. Group A run through 3 gates and exchange with Group D; Group C repeat this with Group B.; then Group A with C, and B with D.

Fig 28 *Evasive running exercises.*

CHAPTER 8
HANDLING

Passing

The type of pass given depends on the spacing between receiver and passer. If close, the ball should be pushed on softly without any spin. The greater the space between passer and receiver, the more weight there has to be behind the pass. Spin will be added to make the ball fly further.

Short Passes

When making a short pass there are certain key factors which should be emphasized. The weight of the pass should be to the far shoulder of the receiver. This means that if the receiver wanted to step into the ball to cut a running line, it would not be so difficult to take. Conversely, if he wanted to drift out, there would be enough weight on the pass for him to take it (on the inside shoulder). This weight of pass gives a receiver more options for his running lines.

The receiver of the pass can help the passer by stretching his arms out and positioning his hands at chest height ready to meet the ball early, and offering a target for the passer. The ball should be kept high. The

> **STAR TIP**
>
> Working hard on the basics is essential; you cannot do enough practising on your passing and catching of a ball.
> Jeremy Guscott
> *(England)*
> *(Rugby World, 1994)*

Lateral Pass

Fig 29   What constitutes a good pass? Run between two stationary players. Player in blue shorts gives the first pass to No. 8. The receiver's hands are ready.

Fig 30   Now give a pass. Swing arms across the body and keep hips square. Evaluate pass out 10.

Fig 31   Passer and receiver evaluate pass. Is there is common agreement?

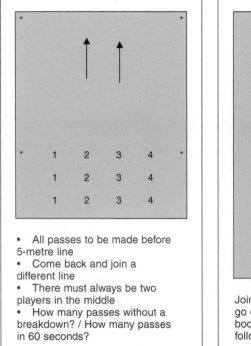

- All passes to be made before 5-metre line
- Come back and join a different line
- There must always be two players in the middle
- How many passes without a breakdown? / How many passes in 60 seconds?

Fig 32   All passes to be made before 5-metre line.

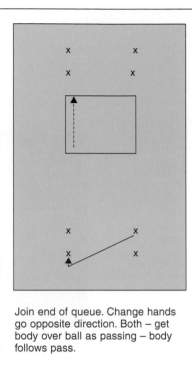

Join end of queue. Change hands go opposite direction. Both – get body over ball as passing – body follows pass.

Fig 33   Long pass.

ball is caught just off the hip at shoulder height. The shortest distance between two points is a straight line. The quickest pass is achieved by raising the elbow of the arm further from the receiver so it is parallel to the ground and pushing the ball out of the hands with palms

and fingers. A pendulum pass, where the ball is brought down from the shoulders and swings in front of the stomach before being released, is slower. In this case, the ball is in the tackle zone and could be clamped by a tackler. If the ball is kept high, an offload over the back of the tackler is still possible.

The running angle for the passer is to fix the defender by running at his inside shoulder. This keeps guard of his own channel and prevents him vacating the channel and drifting on to the receiver of the pass. This means the passer has to pass off the back foot, the foot furthest from the receiver. If he transfers his weight from this back foot to the front foot, it will encourage the defender to drift out.

Spin Pass

For the spin pass over a long distance it is necessary to roll the ball off the palm and the fingertips and roll the wrist over. If the pass is made off the back foot, there will be a tendency to fall away and the ball will be released into the air rather than parallel to the ground. For successful execution of this pass, the forearm, wrist and fingers have to be strong and quick, and the pass can be helped by shifting the body weight from the back to the front foot, getting the upper body over the ball as it is released.

To practise the spin pass, stand still, and throw the ball in the air with spin, so that the ball is propelled upwards in a constant spiral. Use both hands at regular intervals. Stay in the same spot so that the ball lands at the position from which the pass was made. As skill improves, pass the ball higher, always ensuring that accuracy is not lost.

Switch Pass

To change direction, create a hole and catch defenders off-balance, the

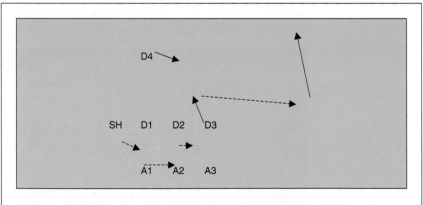

1 passes to 2 who passes to 3 on an unders line busting through the gap. Confronted by defender – gives long pass out to put man clear.

Fig 34   Game situation.

ball carrier runs on a diagonal and, as he takes up the space in front of the receiver, the receiver runs back inside and behind the ball carrier. The ball carrier turns with his back to the opposition. The defenders cannot see the ball, but the receiver can see the ball all the time. He gives a short, soft pass as the receiver is cutting in behind him.

The Loop

One way of supporting the ball carrier after passing, and also a way of creating an extra attacking player, is to pass and loop the ball carrier. For a successful outcome, the player who is being looped should accelerate on to the pass to create space behind him and then step in to create space on the outside. In this way, the looping player delays his run for this to happen and can now get on a straight running line to receive a return pass just off the shoulder of the passer.

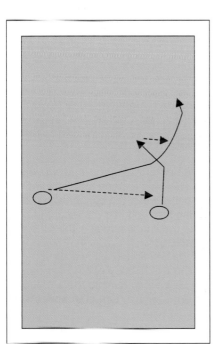

Fig 38 The loop.

Switch Pass

Fig 35 The ball carrier and receiver run diagonally across a grid to opposite corners.

Fig 36 The pass is made as they cross. The ball carrier shields the ball from a defender; the receiver can see the ball all the time.

Fig 37 The next pair go.

Scrum Half Pass

This ball is normally off the ground. If passing to the right, the left foot should be next to the ball and the right foot planted a stride away. The right foot should be pointing towards the receiver with the right knee out of the way. Maintain a wide base and bent knees. Avoid any wind-up. Head and shoulders remain low as the ball is swept away with a wrist action, rolled off the fingertips. Ensure that the follow-through is towards the target. If the follow-through is too long, the passer's left hands will be on ball for too long.

Catching the High Ball

Fig 39   Full back under the high ball: reaching for the ball, good concentration, fingers spread.

Fig 40   Catching – one foot forward to withstand a tackle, elbows in, mark called.

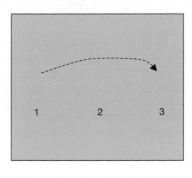

1 throws; 2 catches; 3 with shield gives small dig to receiver after he catches

Fig 41   Catching under pressure.

STAR TIP

When you are catching a high ball, you must do so with your hands above your head. Some players keep their hands down at hip level which means that they cannot guide the ball into the cradle that is formed between the hands and the stomach.

Gavin Hastings
(Scotland)
(Rugby World, 1994)

Catching the High Ball

When chasers are not near, the catcher can take the ball whilst remaining on the ground. It is necessary to get under the ball and keep your eyes on it. Turn slightly to lead with one arm and shoulder and one hip and leg. Spread the fingers, tuck your elbows in, reach up for the ball. As you catch it, pull it into your chest. Call 'My ball' to communicate your intentions. Legs should be at least shoulder width apart, to provide a stable base in case you are tackled at the same time as you make the catch.

If there is a chaser, the player who is under the ball will have to leave the ground in order to get to the ball early. He cannot be tackled whilst he is in the air. He should time leaving the ground so he catches the ball at the top of his jump. If he leads with a knee, this will afford him some protection should the chaser make contact with him. He raises his arms, spreads his fingers, relaxes his palms, which are facing up; he then focuses on the ball, catches it and pulls it down to his chest and arms. There should be two hands on the ball when it hits his chest and the thud of the ball on the chest will be heard.

Lifting the Ball on the Ground

If the ball is stationary, lead with one shoulder and leg and step beyond the ball. Sweep the ball up with the trailing arm and into the leading arm. Bend the knees and sink the hips for a stable base.

If the ball is rolling towards you, get the whole body behind the ball and let the ball roll into the crook of the arms. Again, bend the knees and sink the hips.

Adaptable Handling Drills

Running Lines

Start in a line of four in the corner of a 10 × 10m grid. The ball is at the front of the line. When the ball carrier moves, all step out and arc around. The ball is passed through everyone's hands. Everyone has to be running fast, and the ball has to get to the end within the width of the grid line and before reaching the grid line. Now move to the next corner and move around the grid.

Grid Work

Four groups are arranged around the outside of a 15 × 15m grid. Each player is numbered. Groups A and C run across the grid whilst passing a ball and then change starting places. Then groups D and B go.

The coach calls any two or three or four letters and the nominated groups run across the grid.

The ball starts on the right-hand side of each line. After passing, the first player (1) becomes a defender against his opposite group to stop it scoring – for example, C1 defends against A and A1 defends against C.

The drill develops, with Players 1 and 2 becoming defenders. Now 1 loops to the end of his line and 2 becomes the defender. Then 1 loops and 2 and 3 become defenders.

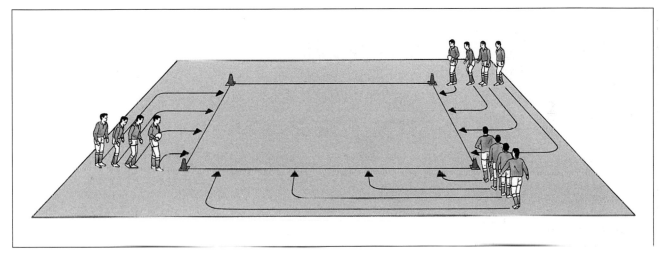

Fig 42   Handling exercise (1) running lines.

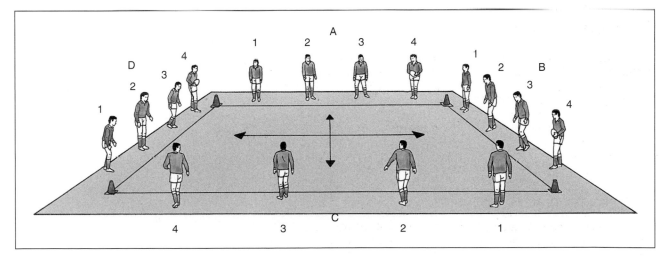

Fig 43   Gridwork.

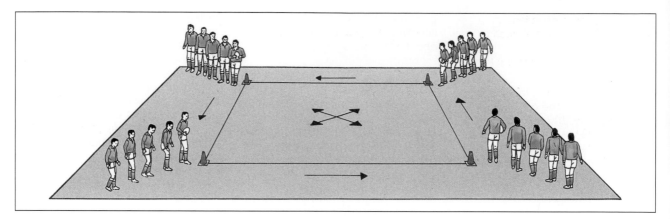

Fig 44   Crossovers.

Crossovers

Using a 10 × 10m grid (Fig 44), five players start in each corner. Each corner has a ball. A ball carrier from each corner runs to the opposite corner and hands on to the next in line.

Give a soft pass, then roll the ball. Now run out 2 metres, place the ball on the ground, run across and lift the ball in the opposite corner, and hand on or give a pop pass. Now the ball carrier runs to the opposite corner but passes to the left (or right) when reaching the middle of the grid.

Circles

This drill is carried out in sevens in a circle. One player stands in the middle. The ball starts on the outside and is passed to the middle player. The passer runs to take his place. The middle player passes to the next player forming the circle and runs to replace him, and he in turn passes to and replaces the middle player.

Narrow Channels

Two lines of players start facing each other (Fig 45). Players run continuously to the right of two cones and pass the ball to a player coming

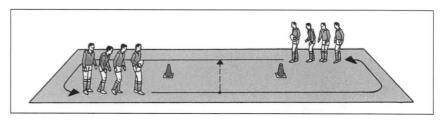

Fig 45   Narrow channels.

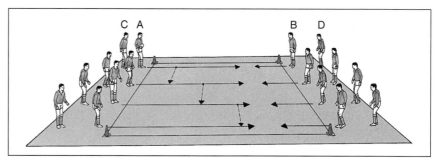

Fig 46   Wide channels.

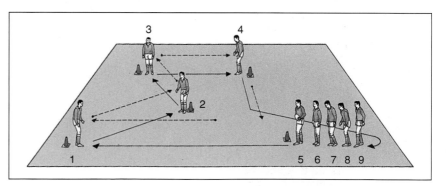

Fig 47   Speed of hand.

from the opposite direction. Develop by adding more balls but pass only to a player without a ball.

Place the ball 5 metres out from each line. The first player in each group runs, dives and gathers in the ball, gets up, runs and places the ball 5 metres away from the opposite line and joins the end of that line.

Develop by changing to a rolling ball and then to a bouncing ball.

Wide Channels

Working along a channel 15 × 10m wide (Fig 41), Group A pass as they run forwards. When it gets to the end player, Group B run forwards and the ball is passed to them. When it gets to the end player, Group C come out and the ball is passed to them.

Decrease the distance between each group. Add miss passes, loops and switch passes.

In a variation, Group A and Group B have a ball. They run at the same time and keep passing. They hand the ball on to the waiting group who then run at the same time.

Speed of Hand

With one player on each cone (Fig 42), Player 5 runs and passes to 1 and follows the pass to take up position 1. Then 1 passes to 2 and follows the pass to take up a new position at 2. Player 2 passes to 3 and follows the pass. When the ball gets to 4, he runs and gives a pop pass to 6, who passes to 1, and the sequence starts all over again. The player from 4 joins the queue.

Develop by including a switch pass from 4 to 5. Now add a standing scrum-half pass from 4 to 5 on the run. Now add another ball to reduce recovery time.

Now add a shield holder between 1 and 5. The first ball carrier runs at the shield and passes to a partner who runs to 1. The player who gave the pass rejoins queue.

Quick Hands!

Fig 48   The middle player throws a ball in the air then receives and gives a pass before catching it.

Fig 49   Passing accurately under pressure. Good concentration and hands ready.

The Scrum Half Pass

Fig 50 The player with the ball passes and follows.

Fig 51 The ball is placed on the ground. The scrum half passes to the next player who puts the ball on the ground.

Fig 52 The third pass is now made.

Fig 53 The next pass is diagonally across the grid. The next player starts.

Scrum-Half Pass

In a 10 × 10m grid with a player in each corner, the acting scrum half makes a pass and follows the ball.

The receiver presents the ball on the ground and the next pass is made. He continues around the grid lines until he gets to the third player, the next pass is across the diagonal.

CHAPTER 9

TACKLING

General Points

The laws of the game define a tackle as occurring when a player who is carrying the ball is held and brought to the ground. The tackled player must play the ball or release it immediately. Both tackler and tackled player must roll away from the ball so that it can become playable.

Effective tackling means flooring the ball carrier so he has to release the ball and is momentarily out of the game. The tackler should aim to end up on top of the tackled player so he can be up and away again before the tackled player. The tackle is made with the shoulder driving through the ball carrier. The spine is in line to transmit the power from the legs through the body. The longer the feet are in contact with the ground, the stronger the driving tackle. The tackler should use his body weight to pull down and use hands to hold on to whatever he can grab.

Crashing front tackles tend to be performed by centres in an area where the players are running flat out at each other. In the midfield, it is a collision sport.

> ### LAWS CHECK
>
> A tackled player must play the ball *immediately* by placing it on or pushing it along the ground or passing it. The tackler must roll away from the ball and the tackled player so that the ball is immediately playable. After the tackle, the next player to play the ball must be on his feet.

Side tackles are usually carried out by outside centres or wings when their opponents are trying an outside break. Covering wings and full backs also use this tackle, as well as the rear tackle.

Front Tackles

Approach the ball carrier quickly, slow slightly to arrive in control and then accelerate into the tackle.

When you launch yourself what you aim at really depends on your own size and your opponent's. Aim between the knees and stomach if the ball carrier is tall and perhaps ungainly. If the ball carrier's hips look strong, the target may have to be below the knees, driving low and up.

If the tackler has little time to get momentum and has to tackle a player who is difficult to knock back, he should crouch low with a wide base and knees bent, drive in at the ball carrier's thighs, absorb the impact, twist and end up on top of the ball carrier.

Fig 54   Front tackle: tackler rides the impact and twists to end up on top.

The Side Tackle

A tackler has to be determined, focus on the point of impact – the thigh – hit with the shoulders and squeeze with the arms. For the sake of safety, the tackler's head should be on the backside and not underneath the tackled player. Both arms encircle the ball carrier. There should be leg drive in contact to win the collision.

The Rear Tackle

The tackler should reach for the waist or top of thigh and slide down both arms, encircling the ball carrier. He should place his head behind the ball carrier.

Tackling Exercises

Drill 1

Body hardness.

Drill 2

Player B stands behind Player A, holding a ball with outstretched arms. The ball is in contact with A's back. Both are jogging forwards. On the signal, B turns and tackles A, who also turns to score on the line behind him.

Develop by B trying to get past A to score on the line in front.

Develop further by allowing Player A to attempt a tackle as soon as the ball is withdrawn from his back.

Drill 3

There are two lines of players: ball carriers and tacklers (Fig 57). On the signal, the first in each line runs into the tackle zone and the ball carrier has to score on the far line.

Drill 1: Body Hardness

Fig 55   Players run through a gate to tackle a free bag.

Fig 56   Pick up the bag and take the place of the bag holder who joins the queue.

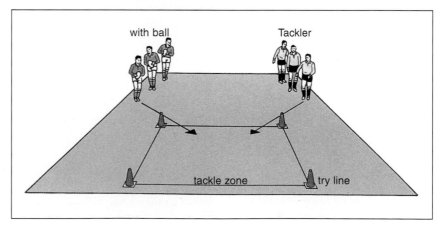

Fig 57   Drill 3.

Drill 4

Using a small grid with four lines of players and two tacklers in the grid (Fig 58), the coach calls direction from which the ball carrier is to come. The ball carrier attempts to join the opposite line and the tacklers try to prevent him.

Drill 5

In groups of six (Fig 59), four remain stationary and pass a ball back and forth. Player A runs behind them and comes through the line at any point, calling for the ball. The tackler B has to prevent him from scoring.

Drill 6

There are two lines of players: one line of tacklers and one line of runners (Fig 60). The runners have to score under the posts and the tacklers have to stop them after running a set course.

Drill 7

Tackle bag drills.

Drill 8

More tackle bag drills.

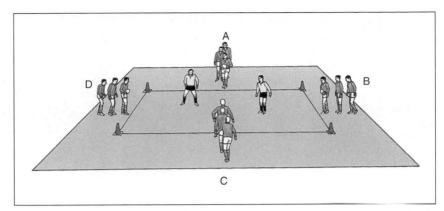

Fig 58   Drill 4.

Fig 59   Drill 5.

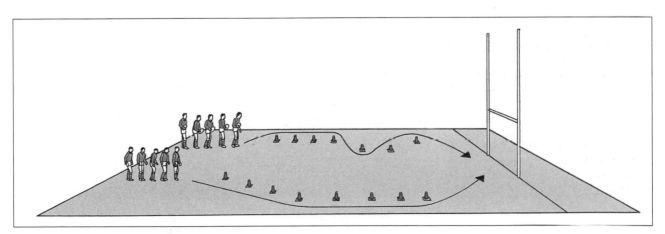

Fig 60   Drill 6.

Drill 7: Tackle Bag Drills

Fig 61   Tackle bag drills are fun!

Fig 62   Tackle bag holder, ball, tackler and support player.

Fig 63   The ball is spilled by the tackler.

Fig 64   The support player retrieves the ball and scores on the next line.

Drill 8: More Tackle Bag Drills

Fig 65   Add another support player.

Fig 66   The ball is spilled and retrieved.

Fig 67   Bring the ball back towards the starting line to score.

CHAPTER 10

KICKING

Kicking has a huge part to play in the game of rugby union and yet rarely is it taught well. Coaches often leave their specialist kickers to go off and practise on their own, but really kicking should be an integral part of a training session for all players.

There is a wide variety of kicks, some strategic and some tactical. The strategic kicks are place kicks at goal (penalties or conversions), the drop-out restarts from half-way and the 22-metre line, which can be long or short (requiring different techniques), the drop-goal, punting (either the spiral or the end-over-end punt), and the bomb (or 'up-and-under').

The tactical kicks are the ones taken by ball carriers who decide to use these manoeuvres to get behind defences. The grubber is stabbed through for a runner, and the chip kick may be a diagonal one for a team-mate or for the kicker himself. The cross-field kick and the scrum-half box kick fall into both categories.

There are a number of advantages in kicking: it is a simple tactic to use; it pressurizes and turns the opposition; and it helps the kicking team to go forward. However, a team must realize that poorly executed kicks can allow the opposition the opportunity of counter-attacking. The tactic also becomes null and void into a strong wind.

Strategy

Teams should have a kicking strategy. The players should know the reasons why they are kicking, from where, by whom, and what type of kick they will

LAWS CHECK

A player is off side if he is in front of a team mate who is carrying the ball, or who kicked the ball. An offside player must retire towards his own goal-line until put on side. He can be put on side in three ways:
• he runs behind the team mate who last played the ball
• the ball carrier runs ahead of him
• when a team mate who was behind the kicker runs in front of the player who was offside.

Fig 68   Stephen Myler, fly half and specialist kicker.

The Punt

Fig 69   Hands underneath both ends of the ball; ball angled across the body.

Fig 70   Head down, tight left shoulder.

Fig 71   Follow through left hand to right foot.

use. There are a few good reasons for kicking: to gain territory; to expose a weakness at full back, for example; as an attacking set move with chasers; to get the forwards going forward; and as a safety-first measure, to avoid mistakes.

Punting

End-Over-End Punt

The ball is held slightly outside the line of the body at waist height. The hands release the ball at the same time so that it drops in the perfect position. The kicking foot has the toe pointing forwards at the ground. The head must stay down and over the ball. The whole body drives forwards so it finishes ahead of the kicking point. The plant foot, the kicking foot and the body should be square on to the target.

Spiral Punt

The ball should be held in the correct position. For a right-footed kicker the angle across the body will be 11 o'clock (left hand) and 5 o'clock (right hand). The spiral comes from this angle as it makes contact with the foot. The hands release to the side to allow the ball to drop correctly on to the foot. The top of the foot makes contact with the belly of the ball with the toes pointing downwards. The head is kept down and over the ball.

Follow through – left foot, right hand and finish beyond the starting point facing the target.

Place Kick

The ball is placed on the tee with the seam lined up with the middle of the posts. The point of contact is below the centre of the ball, making sure that the strike is not too low, as the result will be back spin and reduced distance. The non-kicking foot should be opposite the ball and about 30cm

(12in) away. A long run-up does not generate more power. The power in the strike comes from the last step. A bigger step generates more power than a shorter one, but there is a point at which the last step becomes too long and the power decreases. The kicker comes straight on to the ball. The standing foot points towards the target and the head should be kept down and over the ball. The foot chases the ball through straight. The kicking foot remains aimed at the posts, even after the strike. End up in front of the kicking point with the body pointing towards the target. The chest should be square on to the ball.

KEY POINT

Place kicking points:
• spot place the ball, and concentrate on the piece of stitching you intend to kick
• line up the seam of the ball, aiming at the target
• the follow through has to be straight, 15cm after the ball
• as you walk back say 'spot, line, follow through'. Look up, imagine the ball going over. Then do it.

Drop-Kicking – Restarts

The short kick restart, with as long as possible hang time, is the usual requirement to allow chasers to get to the ball in order to regain possession. Hold each side of the ball near the bottom, at about knee height and close to the body. Stand in a slightly crouched position. Head and shoulders remain square to the intended target area. The body is over the ball, and the kicker is leaning forwards. The non-kicking leg bends as the ball hits the ground, which allows the ball to be struck on the foot's upward curve. The toes of the kicking foot come back slightly towards the leg; they are not extended. There is a flick of the foot so that the ball rises high.

The Place Kick

Fig 72   Use the seam of the ball to aim it at the posts.

Fig 73   Starting position: plant foot level with the ball; measure the same run up each time for consistency.

Fig 74   Arm out for balance; keep the shoulder in tight. If it swings out, it pulls the hips out and the foot will swing across the ball and not through it.

Fig 75   Head down and follow through.

Chip Kick

Fig 76   Ball carrier comes out at same time as defender from opposite line. Chip over. Do not get too close; high knee action to maintain running speed.

Fig 77   Catch.

Fig 78   Hand on to player waiting.

Drop-Kicking at Goal

This kick is similar to the long restart kick but with more pressure because defenders are trying to charge it down. The ball is held away from the body to allow a longer final step, which in turn generates more power from the back lift of the kicking leg. The ball is angled slightly back. The hands hold the sides of the ball. The kicker aims to make contact early; his action is to go through the ball for distance. The ball does not come up from the ground before the strike. The non-kicking foot points to the target. Shoulders are square and the weight goes forwards. Follow through. Catch the ball on the kicking foot side of the body to saves time wasted by any readjustment that would otherwise be needed.

The Chip

The chip kick is similar to the end-over-end punt but the toes point upwards and the body leans forwards.

The Grubber

The ball is held pointing away from the body and belly down. The kicker drives the ball into the ground with the top of the foot; the further away from him this occurs, the longer the ball will travel. The ball will bounce end over end.

The Scrum-Half Box Kick

The box kick is executed from a scrum, ruck or maul, or a driven ball from a lineout. It is essential to get the ball high for a distance of no more than about 25 metres. It is usually executed within 10–15 metres from the right touch-line (for a right-footed kick). Accuracy is the key. There must be a call for this kicking option, as it has to be chased if it is to be properly utilized.

The scrum half places the ball under the cross-bar and on the goal-

Grubber Kick

Fig 79   Score goals; hold the ball upright to make it bounce end over end.

Fig 80   Fielding the ball: whole body in front of the ball, bend knees, allow ball to roll into the crook of the arms.

line between the posts. He takes a step back and box-kicks the ball over the cross-bar to land 15–20 metres downfield.

The kicker starts with a reasonably wide base and takes just one step sideways and backwards. He should hold the ball in the palm of his hand at approximately a 45-degree angle. Contact is made underneath the ball, sending it end over end. The leg follows through as high as possible with a smooth action. Avoid stabbing the ball. Holding the ball higher helps the kicker to gain extra distance. This means there will be a larger swing and the kicker must ensure that he kicks up and through the ball. The

head must be kept down as long as possible; it is a common fault in kickers to bring the head up too soon, to see where the ball has gone. The kicker should finish with his chest facing towards the touch-line rather than facing forwards down the pitch. This is to avoid the kick travelling too far and flat.

Kicking Exercises

Exercise 1

Kicking tennis: a game with several balls and two or three players each side. Each team is in a 10 × 10m

grid, with a 20-metre grid between them. They punt to each other non-stop and achieve a score if the ball lands in the defended zone. If the ball is caught, there is no score and there is no score either for a ball landing outside the zone. The winning team is the first to score ten.

Exercise 2

Two groups are lined up opposite each other about 10 metres apart. The first player from Group A has the ball and runs out towards Group B. The first in Group B runs out with hands held high to challenge the ball carrier. The ball carrier chips

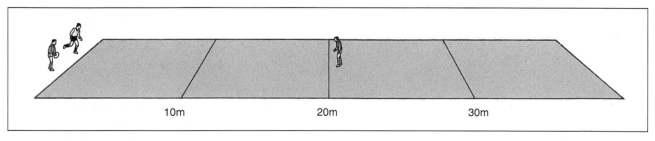

10m   20m   30m

Fig 81   Kicking exercises – the bomb.

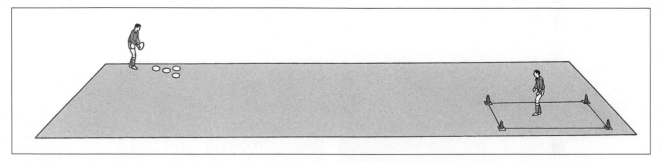

Fig 82 The scrum half box kick.

the ball over him and runs on to retrieve it. He gives the ball to the first player in Group B, and joins the end of the queue as his challenger joins the end of Group A. The process restarts with the ball carrier from B being challenged by the player at the front of A.

Exercise 3

Set out two sets of goal-posts with cones with one or two goalkeepers to each goal. Grub kick at the opposition goal from your own goal mouth to score. Try to stop them scoring as if you were a soccer goalkeeper. The first side to ten goals wins.

Exercise 4

The kicker practises short restarts by kicking over the posts as close as he can get. This will encourage him to get under the ball. He gradually moves further back.

Exercise 5

Using a 10 × 10m grid and two lines of players, one line in each of two corners, the kicker chips (or grub kicks) into the corner for a chaser to gather and score. They swap places.

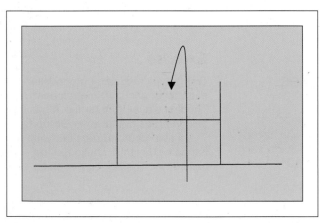

Fig 83 Exercise 4 (Drop Kick restart)

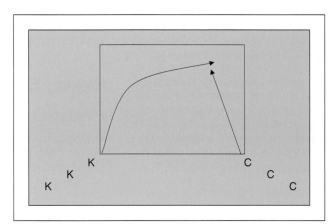

Fig 84 Exercise 5 (Diagonal chip kick)

PART 4

SET PLAYS

CHAPTER 11

THE SCRUM

Relevant Laws

In the interests of safety in scrummaging, different laws operate at various age groups. The laws for the senior game have been changed over a number of years, also in the interests of safety. Each front row must have three players. Before they engage, they must be an arm's length away and the scrum half should have the ball in his hands. This prevents the two packs charging at each other, and means that the two packs are not scrummaging for so long before the ball is available to be put in. Before engagement, the referee shouts, 'Crouch, touch, pause, engage', with similar intentions of preparing everyone for the impact.

Each player in the front row must be in a pushing position, with both feet on the ground and shoulders above hips to prevent any collapse. Front-row players are not allowed to kick the ball through the scrum, collapse the scrum, lift an opponent out of the scrum, or handle the ball in the scrum. These are all potentially dangerous activities.

The scrum half's actions are governed by a number of laws. He must put the ball in straight down the middle of the tunnel formed by the two front rows. He must stand 1 metre from the tunnel. The ball has to touch the ground beyond the width of the loose-head prop's shoulders. The scrum half is not allowed to dummy a pass from the base of the scrum.

The offside line for players not in the scrum (the threequarters) is the hindmost foot of the hindmost player in the scrum. The opposing scrum half is the exception and can follow the ball, although he must not get in front of it. The scrum must not wheel more than 90 degrees; if this happens, a new scrum is ordered.

No scrum may be formed fewer than 5 metres from the touch-line, nor in the in-goal area. If a scrum is pushed back over the goal-line, the scrum has ended and a player may ground the ball. If a defender does this another attacking scrum is ordered, 5 metres out. An attacking player doing this scores a try.

Advantages of Scrummaging

Possession of the ball from scrums is generally assured. If the scrums are stable, they can be used as a platform for a back-row attack. The best-quality ball is achieved when the scrum is moving forwards and the ball is delivered at that moment. This means that the opposition back row cannot be so effective in defence. By pressurizing the opposition ball, the scrum can be a means of denying the opposition quality possession.

A dominant scrum can exhaust the opposition forwards, both mentally and physically. In an attempt to sap the energy of the opposition, teams such as France and Argentina have experimented with pushing over the ball, rather than having the front row striking for the ball. The collective push can capture the ball, but it fails, of course, when the opposition front row is bigger and stronger.

Key Factors in Scrummaging

Safety Measures

Correct Technique

Players are to be encouraged to build up their strength and flexibility, particularly around the neck and shoulders.

All forwards should be made aware of safety in scrummaging. The correct scrummaging technique is similar to the weight-lifting position: head and chin up, legs bent, straight back, hips square, feet shoulder width apart and pointing forwards. Head and shoulders must be above the hips.

KIT CHECK

Shin guards are recommended for the front row players.

Evasive Actions

If the chin is pressed to the chest, and the neck is turned until the chin is close to the shoulder, the player is in a dangerous position. His neck may even be broken if any weight is then applied downwards by the scrum collapsing.

If a scrum collapses, players should drop on to their knees before their head hits the ground. They should release their arms to absorb the weight on their elbow and forearm. This position is relatively safe. The second row must stop pushing.

Neck Strengthening Exercise in Pairs

Fig 85 Pulling the head forwards to force the chin on to the chest.

Fig 86 Pushing on the forehead.

Scrummaging Efficiency

Scrummaging requires concentration to achieve efficiency. All forwards must be focused, know their individual roles and work together. The props protect their hooker and transmit the power generated by the second row, the locks and flankers. The No.8 binds the locks together.

There are several forces working in different directions in the scrum. Applying force in the right direction at the correct times requires the co-ordination of the whole pack. The forces are circular (going around or wheeling); horizontal (forward drive and going backwards); and vertical (going up and down).

Body Positions

The correct body position can generate power or resist the opposition's drive. Power comes from the thighs, calves and contact of the feet with the ground and is transmitted through the back. The feet should be a shoulder width apart. The toes point forwards. The back is hollow, the stomach out, the spine in line, the chin up. The body is straight and square on a line down the nose and through the centre of the body.

The power of the legs can be generated into explosive power only if the knee is bent. If it is slightly bent, there will only be a small, but quick movement forwards. If it is a deep bend, the forward movement will be slow, but further. Straight legs prevent players going backwards but there is no forward movement. A compromise is a vertical thigh with an angle of about 120 degrees between the thigh and the calf.

The Loose-Head Ball: Own Put-In

The Front Row

The front row delivers the force initiated by the rest of the pack. The loose-head prop binds first on his hooker on his own put-in. Both props

---

LAWS CHECK

A player must not intentionally collapse the scrum or lift an opponent up and out of the scrum.

KEY POINT

Scrummaging is a mental exercise. Concentrate on getting hips square; keeping strong grips; chin up and a firm upper body.

KEY POINT

The front row is responsible for the transfer of weight from behind into the opposition. It must give a platform for the players behind.

STAR TIP

The more muscles you can develop
in the neck and shoulders, the less
chance of injury. You can do a
simple exercise in which a friend
tries to resist as you push and pull
your neck into all angles.

Jason Leonard
(England)
(Rugby World, 1995)

square up their shoulders by pushing
their inside shoulder through.

All hips are kept at the same
height and parallel. To push upfield
and transmit the forces being
generated, the hips of the props
should be square. If all feet point
forwards, it will keep the hips square.

The hips, shoulder and feet should
be the same width. The heels should
be as close to the ground as
possible. All forwards should work
hard on flexibility in the regions of
the hamstrings, calves and Achilles
tendons.

The thigh of the inside leg of the
props should be vertical, to provide a
surface for the second row to push
on. If the knee is in front of the hip,
the knee will buckle when pressure
is applied. If the knee is too far back,
the flankers will ride up over the back
of the props.

Loose-Head Prop

The loose-head prop has three
objectives: to maintain his binding
with his hooker; ensure the hooker
gets a clear view of the ball as it
comes in; and transmit the force
generated from behind. He binds on
the hooker with the right arm. The
grip will be high up and above the arm
of his tight head. He should not bind
on the hooker's hips because this will
restrict the hooker's hip movement
when he strikes for the ball.

The prop's feet are behind his
shoulders, the heels of the outside
foot being level with the toes of the

inside leg. The left foot has to be
slightly forward to create the channel
for the ball when the hooker strikes,
but not too far forward that the prop
cannot support weight and also
transmit it forwards. His inside foot
will be behind the hooker's left foot.
Feet should be shoulder width apart
for stability and pointing upfield
parallel to touch.

He brings the inside shoulder and
hips square and makes contact with
the opposition with the right shoulder.
He engages from below, coming up,
in the crouched position, bending
forwards and not exposing any of the
chest. His weakness is the upper
arm when engaging so he should get
his left arm over the back of the
tight-head prop. His elbow must be
up, otherwise it might interfere with
the hooker's view of the ball coming
in. He clenches the fist and rolls the
arm up. A high elbow tenses the
shoulder and neck muscles.

Tight-Head Prop

The tight-head prop steps in behind
the hooker and grips the hooker near

the waist. He brings his left shoulder
through and square. At engagement,
the tight-head should be straight on
when he binds with his hooker. If he
tries to drive across to attack the
opposing hooker's binding with his
loose-head, he will leave his chest
exposed to the loose-head, who will
attempt to get his head under his
chest. It will also mean that his hips
are pointing to the middle of the
tunnel, and this may involve a danger
of being twisted by pressure from
behind and in front.

The Hooker

The hooker binds over both of his
props. This brings him closer to the
middle of the tunnel; both props will
be able to hold his weight, leaving his
leg free for hooking; and the front row
will be closely bound.

The loose-head binds first, high up
on the hooker. The tight-head prop
binds low on the hooker. this gives
the right side of the hooker's body
greater manoeuvrability. The right
side can sink and twist, and the hip
can move closer to the ball.

Fig 87   Front row binding: loose head prop binds high on the hooker; tight head prop binds low.

To allow the locks to get their head in, the hooker should move his hips forwards. The props should not move theirs.

The hooker leads in with the right shoulder and right hip so that the top half of his body faces the ball. If he goes in square, he may not be able to hook. His weight should be on his left leg and shoulder.

His toes and knees point towards the outside shoulder of the opposite tight-head prop. The toes of the right foot should be on the ground. As the ball is put in, the hooker strikes beyond the ball, diagonally forward and across to the left, and hooks it with the instep of his right foot or the back of the foot or lower calf. The outside of the right foot sweeps across the ground. The draw back should not hit the left foot.

The hooker strikes as soon as the ball leaves the scrum half's hands. The scrum half puts in the ball when the signal is given by the hooker. The generally accepted method of signalling is for the hooker to lift his left hand from his loose-head and to tap the loose-head at the moment when he wants the ball put in.

Only the hooker strikes for the ball. Only when the ball is put in on the tight-head side will the props try to help the hooker win the ball.

The Second Row

The second row consists of the two locks and the two flankers. Their aims are to generate power to the front row and prevent a retreating scrum.

The Locks

The locks should bind together before binding with the front row. The right lock would be the taller of the two locks, to help counter-act the natural wheeling tendency of the scrum. He will bind over the shoulder of his partner. This allows him to pull his left shoulder through and get it square.

His body will then be straight and his right shoulder will be in a better position to transmit the power from his legs to the tight-head.

If the locks grip high on each other, around the armpit, the binding is tighter at the shoulders and keeps the front row tight. If the binding is low, on the shorts, the locks are kept straight because it means that the shoulders of the two locks can be kept in one line. There must still be space at the hips to allow the No.8 to get his head between them.

The locks should bind on to the props with their outside arm through the legs of their respective props.

The left lock's binding on the loose-head should be his left arm reaching towards his own left ear and gripping the waistband of the prop's shorts, that is, through and across the groin. The angle of the arm means that it is a short and, therefore, strong lever. If the lock binds through the legs and on to the top of the shorts, there is a danger of pulling the prop down.

Although binding around the prop's

Fig 88   The locks binding on each other.

Fig 89   The lock binding on the front row. The hooker pushes his hips forwards to let the locks get their head in.

Fig 90   Left lock binding on to loose head prop: through the legs, hand reaches towards own left ear and grabs the waist band.

Fig 91   Square hips and spine in line.

hips is used for midi rugby, in which scrums are uncontested, it is not recommended at senior level. This method pulls the front row together, but there will be little room for the flankers to push on the props. The lock's shoulders could also slide up over the top of the prop's hips and on to his back.

The point of the shoulder should be under the prop's tailbone to transfer weight through his pelvis and spine. If it is any lower, the knee will buckle. The left lock's emphasis will be on his left shoulder and the right lock on his right shoulder so that the hooker is not impeded.

If they start with a vertical back and go into a locked position with legs straight and no knee bend, the locks must sink and bend their knees to push. In the act of sinking to bend their knees, their head and shoulders retreat and they are nudged backwards. It is better to start with a high back in a crouched position with the backside about an inch higher than the shoulders. The feet should be further forward so that, when they sink the hips to parallel by dipping the knees, their shoulders are edged forwards and up, and the scrum goes forwards. The locks have their feet back and a shoulder width apart; this will give them the stability needed to apply power. Feet should be pointing upfield with heels as close to the ground as possible, putting all the drive in one line. Give and receive pressure over the knee joints and keep the feet still. If the feet are splayed to give greater grip on the ground, it means that the inside of the knee is facing the ground. This will prevent a drive but there will be great pressure on the knee.

The Flankers

The flankers try to generate power and keep the scrum square by helping the props. They bind on to the back of their respective locks with the inside arm. If the flankers are square and parallel to the locks, they can transmit their power to the props. Their pushing shoulders need to be in contact with the prop under his tailbone, to transfer weight through his pelvis and spine. The left flanker's neck, side of the face and the other arm can be used to keep in the loose-head prop's hips. The inside leg should be back, with the outside foot forward. The flankers push off both legs but the emphasis is largely off the inside of the outside foot.

Both flankers should be able to see into the scrum to identify what has happened to the ball and be able to react to the situation.

The No.8

The third row is the No.8, who can pack in one of two places: between the locks (Channel 2) or between the left flanker and left lock (Channel 1). At U19 level, he can only pack down in Channel 2.

The No.8 binds around the hips of the two locks, gripping the top of their shorts. His shoulders will be below the tailbone of the locks. Both feet will be back and level, with his weight on his left foot to enable him to control the ball with his right foot.

Fig 92   The flankers binding on: hips are square to contribute to the forward drive.

Engaging the Opposition

All players involved in the scrum bind together before engaging, except the No.8, who is permitted to get down later to have longer to survey the field and anticipate what options are available. If there is sufficient communication, cohesion will be achieved. Either the hooker or the tight head will call the scrum in. He may, for example, say, 'Sink, down and weight', or, 'Squeeze, knees, in.'

The hooker controls the height of the scrum and the distance from the opposition front row at which they will start their engagement. If they are too near or too far away, they will have to move again after the engagement to get into the correct position, which causes disruption. If the front row starts too far away, it stumbles forwards and down, the props overreach and this swings their hips out; if they are too close, there will be an inadequate drive.

Bend forwards rather than crouching, to prevent the chest being exposed. The second row drives the front row into the opposition.

Props, locks and flankers need to get their weight on the balls of the feet, in the sprint position. This will give them extra inches in the engagement. The front row ripples in to counter the natural wheeling tendency of the scrum. The tight-head prop starts with his feet and shoulders in front of his own loose-head prop's. He leads with the inside shoulder to keep the hips square. The right lock and right flanker drive him further forwards. This also pushes the hooker's hips and feet closer to the tunnel entrance.

The props should never straighten their legs. If the props push, the flat pushing platform goes for the locks.

Stability and control can be achieved through good body positions. Keep the shoulders and hips square, the chin up, and a hollow back. Squeeze with a strong grip, and roll the wrists over. All players need to get right with the men in front, then tighten up on men next to them.

The knees are bent ready to explode into action and the upper body should be tensed.

Fig 93   Front row prior to engagement: crouched low with little of the chest exposed to the opposition.

Fig 94   The forwards packed down: hips and feet point forwards; knees bent; tight binding.

side of the scrum, for the ball to emerge between the left flanker and left lock. It is the quickest path to get the ball out of the scrum and away.

Channel 2: either (a) the ball goes through the loose-head prop's legs to the left flanker. He controls it with the inside of his right foot and then puts the ball across to the No.8 through the locks with the outside of his right foot. Alternatively, (b) the loose-head prop moves his right foot from behind the hooker. The hooker strikes deeper towards his tight-head prop and hits the ball with his heel. The ball is taken from the left side to the right-hand side of the scrum through the space between his left foot and the loose-head prop's right foot, through the locks. The left lock moves his left foot over and the ball emerges by the right foot of the No.8, who has to play football with it.

The Drive

Before the put-in, the forwards must squeeze hard on their bindings and lower their knees. When the ball goes in, they should drive through their thighs and back to win a few inches.

Attacking from a Scrum

The Options

The off-side line for the opposing backs is an imaginary line running at right-angles across the field through the hindmost foot of the scrum. The opposing backs are so close that it is difficult to launch attacks through the threequarters. The other attacking option is to kick. The scrum half can kick the ball into the box in front of the forwards, when the scrum is about 15 metres in from the touch-line. The nearest winger and inside centre will then give chase. From a midfield scrum, the fly half might kick to the corners. Back-row moves are

The Put-In

The hooker controls the timing of the entry of the ball by signalling to the scrum half when he wants the ball in.

The scrum half holds the ball with its long axis parallel to the ground and the right end of the ball pointing towards the hooker. If the opposition hooker gets to the ball, contact will be unfavourable.

The ball is pitched just beyond the loose-head prop's head. Channel 1: the hooker strikes the ball through the loose-head's legs down the left another option from a scrum. The objectives are to cross the gain-line early and to engage the opposition back-row forwards to take them out of the game.

Back-Row Moves: Conditions

A stable forward platform is a prerequisite to launch an attack through the back row. There must be one back-row player who is powerful and quick enough to drive across the gain-line. Speed of execution is essential. The opposition must be given little time in which to react, to organize a shove or break their binding to get away and defend.

The whole pack has to work hard to wheel the scrum; to get the side advanced that needs to be slightly ahead of the other. If you are attacking to the right, try to get the tight-head prop in front of his loose-head thus making it harder for the opposition flanker to defend against the No.8 who is picking up.

It is usual to attack to the right of scrums for a couple of reasons: the defending scrum half is on the left side and the attacking side should have an advantage in numbers; and it is easier to build up momentum as the ball goes from left to right in the scrum to the No.8's feet and the scrum half is moving quickly to it.

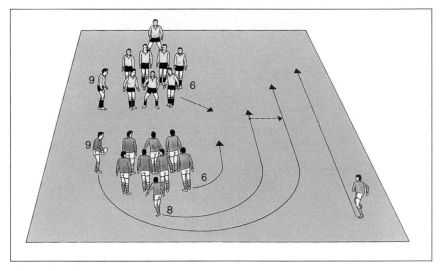

Fig 95   Move 1.

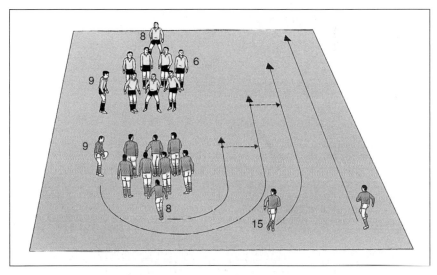

Fig 96   Move 2.

Back-Row Moves: Examples

Move 1

Field position: 15–30m from right touch-line.

Players' movements: No. 8 picks up moving from left to right close to scrum. Draws opposing No.6 and passes to scrum half arcing in same direction.

Passing options: outside to right wing or inside to flanker.

Development: the No. 8 picks up and runs on a wider arc to make room on the inside for a pass back to the right flanker. The right flanker now passes out to the scrum half going wide.

Move 2

Field position: 30m from right touch-line.

Players' movements: No.8 picks up moving from left to right close to scrum. Draws opposing No.6 and passes to scrum half arcing in same direction. Scrum half fixes the opposing No.8 and gives a flat pass to the full back.

Passing options: outside to right wing or inside to flanker.

Move 3

Field position: 15 to 35m from left touch-line. 25m from their goal-line.

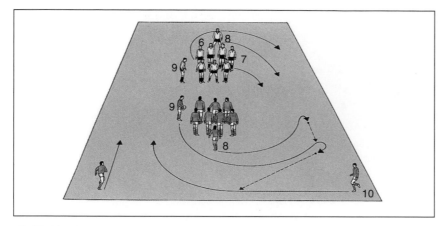

Fig 97   Move 3.

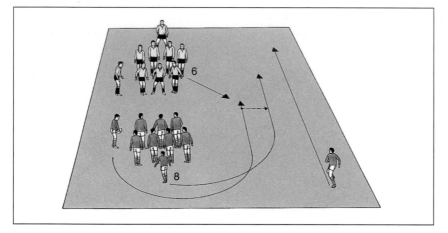

Fig 98   Move 4.

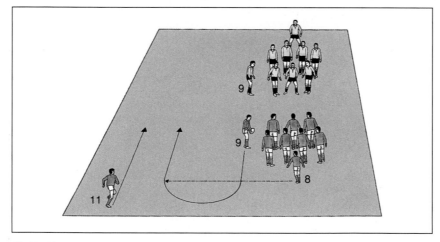

Fig 99   Move 5.

Players' movements: No.8 picks up moving left to right. Stops 5m wide of the scrum on the right to give a pass to the scrum half who gives a pass to the fly half, moving right to left on a flat run to the left of the scrum.

Passing options: outside to left wing or inside to blind-side flanker.

Move 4

Field position: minimum 15 metres from right touch-line.

Players' movements: scrum half picks up from base and moves left to right close to scrum. He takes out opposing No.6 passing to No.8 looping on arc in same direction.

Passing options: outside to right wing or inside to flanker.

Development: scrum half picks up going wide and passes back inside to No.8.

Move 5

Field position: 10–30m from left touch-line.

Players' movements: No.8 in Channel 1. Scrum half puts in and quickly drops back to left of scrum. No.8 feeds scrum half from base. Scrum half runs up the left channel.

Passing options: outside to left wing or inside to blind-side flanker.

Move 6

Field position: 10 to 30m from left touch-line and 30m from opposition goal-line.

Players' movements: No.8 in Channel 1 and No.7 in Channel 2. Scrum half moves to base of scrum. No.8 picks up and backs into opposing scrum half going left. Right flanker binds over his outside shoulder and No.6 binds over inside shoulder.

'Drive': the left lock drives in on the ball to create a driving maul.

'Feed': No.8 passes to the left lock moving right to left. Passing options: outside to left wing or to other lock or inside to back row.

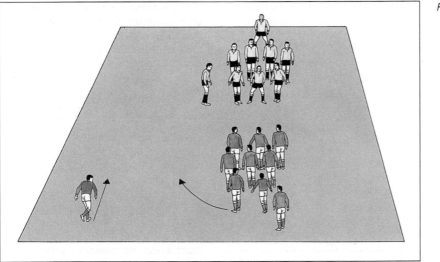

Fig 100   Move 6.

Fig 101 (a)   Move 6.

Fig 101 (b)   Move 6.

Move 7

Field position: Midfield.

Players' movements: scrum half passes to centre on the right of the scrum. The centre runs diagonally back towards the opposing flanker. He switches with the No. 8 (1), who passes to the scrum half (2). The scrum half passes to the full back in close and on the burst.

Passing options: on outside to winger and on inside to back row.

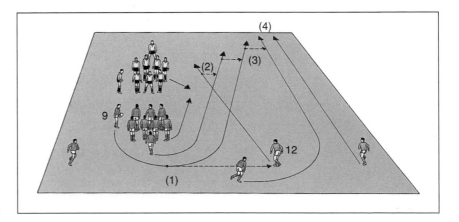

Fig 102   Move 7.

The Tight-Head Ball: The Opposition Put-In

Objectives

When the opposition are putting the ball in, the aim of the defending pack of forwards is either to win the ball by hooking it, or to disrupt the opposition ball so much that they cannot launch an effective attack.

The Heel Against the Head

The hooker should be selective about when to strike for the tight-head ball. He will only attempt it two or three times in a match. It may be deep in defence to rob the opposition of a strong attacking position, or it may be deep in the opposition half to win the ball in a possible scoring position. He must communicate with the rest of his pack if he does make a decision to attempt the strike.

The hooker binds over the tight-head prop's shoulders and on to waist of the loose-head prop and under his arm. His right buttock faces the tunnel entrance. His weight is on his left leg.

The hooker has to watch the opposition hooker's foot to know when to strike. He strikes behind the hooker's foot with his right foot or he strikes diagonally across and over the opposing hooker's right leg, hoping to deflect it back with the outside of the foot or heel.

The tight-head prop contributes by putting his left foot behind the hooker and bearing his weight on it. He can then use his right foot to help in hooking the ball after the hooker has made contact with it.

The rest of the pack drive forwards on the signal from the flanker ('Ready, now').

Eight-Man Shove

To disrupt the opposition ball by making them retreat, all the forwards drive straight. There is no overlap of feet between the hooker and the props. Locks now shove on the hooker, who is also square and ready to drive. The right flanker gives the signal when to drive.

Defence of Back Row from a Scrum

The two flankers and No.8 and scrum half deal with their opposite mini unit. Communication is important. The No.8 is the last to get down. He has a look around to see what the opposition intend to do. He communicates what he has identified to the rest of the back row. The scrum half must then communicate to his back row when the ball is out, so that the back row can detach and defend.

Defending the Narrow Side on the Left Side of the Field

The blind-side flanker (No. 6) takes the first player around on his side of the scrum, usually the scrum half or No.8. He must go forwards to prevent the opposition crossing the gain-line. The No.8 takes the second player around the scrum.

The open-side flanker covers back behind the line of the No.8. If he follows the ball around the attackers' side of the scrum when a breakdown occurs, he will be on the wrong side of it and unable to contribute. He should aim to get between the ball and his own goal-line.

Defending the Open-Side on the Left Side of the Field

The Scrum Half is responsible for the first man around and the open-side flanker takes the second man. The No.7 can be prepared to pressurize their outside half because their scrum half is covered by the scrum half.

The No.8 covers just behind the No.7 and takes any player cutting back inside the open-side flanker. The blind-side flanker first checks his own side then covers behind the scrum and behind the No.8.

Defending the Open-Side on the Right Side of the Field

The No.7 goes to the left side of the scrum and takes the first man around. The No.8 takes the second man around.

The attacking fly half gets a bit more time with a scrum on this side of the field because the defending open-side flanker has first to check that there is no one coming around the scrum before pressurizing the fly half.

Defending the Narrow Side on the Right Side of the Field

The scrum half will cover the first man around with the blind-side flanker covering the second man around.

Defending a Midfield Scrum

If the attack is coming left, the No.6 packs left and takes the first man, with the No.8 taking the second man and the No.7 covering deep. If the attack is coming right, the scrum half takes the first man around and No.7 the second man. If the first man is the outside half, the scrum half will go for him and will not be putting so much pressure on the attacking scrum half.

Exercises

Warm-Up

To strengthen neck and shoulders, get in pairs on hands and knees and in a pushing position. Push against each other in turn, with flat back and head under chest. One will lift the other by pushing up his chin. Now take the knees about 7.5cm (3in) off the ground. Then do the same in a higher position, with firm feet and strong binding.

Body Position

In pairs and kneeling, the knees are shoulder width apart. Torso and thighs are at right-angles, toes on ground. Chin up, hollow base. Arm over partner's neck and shoulders. Rhythmic rocking back and forth. Push forwards from backside and thighs. Do not scrummage from the shoulders. Look forwards. Gradually start to resist each other. Where do you feel it when there is resistance? Change binding arm; then bind with both arms, left under and right over.

Lift knees off ground slightly. Dig in toes. Look forwards. Do not pull down. Lower and lift by 7.5 or 15cm (3 or 6in) using scrummage position of heads under chests.

Co-ordination

Exercise 1: for timing, all get in a circle and hold on to each other. On the command 'Ready, Ready, Now', all jump into the air, still holding on.

Exercise 2: two packs for thirty-second intervals move forwards, backwards, sideways, sink, come up, on the coach's command.

The Put-In and Hook

Hooker leans on right hand and scrum half rolls ball for him to hook. To sharpen up the hooker's strike, the scrum half drops the ball and the hooker has to hit it on the half-volley. Now, as the scrum half drops the ball from varying heights, the hooker tries to sweep under the ball before it bounces.

Loose-Head Prop

Using two front rows, the loose-head prop synchronizes driving upwards

when the scrum half puts in the ball, alternating between Channel 1 and Channel 2, so the loose-head prop and hooker can make the necessary foot adjustments.

Tight-Head Prop

The tight-head against two opponents drives forwards and upwards. Then he retreats and counter-attacks.

The Locks

Three against five (or six against eight). Locks and No.8 in a three-man scrum against three plus two. The pressure can be increased by taking away the No. 8.

Back Row

To establish lines of run, have a line of four players behind a grid. On the signal they are to arc around, passing the ball to the end player before they cross a grid-line and within the distance of the grid marker.

Now add a defensive problem, three against two.

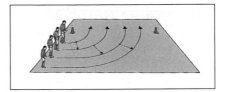

Fig 103(a)   Back row.

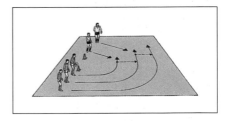

Fig 103(b)   Back row – three players against two.

Defending the left-hand corner: attacking back row and scrum half and right wing against defending back row and scrum half and left wing. Defenders start on knees initially.

Back rows and two scrum halfs get in their usual formation in the scrum. Coach arranges the feeds. The attacking back row goes through its moves and the defending side organizes its defences.

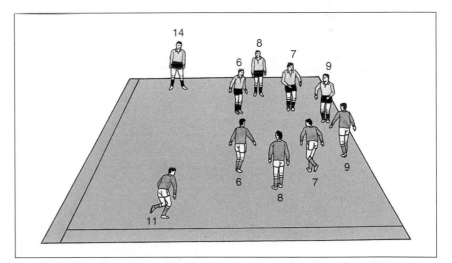

Fig 104   Back row. Defending the left-hand corner of the grid.

CHAPTER 12

THE LINEOUT

Relevant Laws

There are more laws concerning the lineout than any other aspect of the game. Referees are generally looking to see that the jumpers are not impeded, that the off-side line is observed, and that the advantage law is applied.

For the ball to be in touch, the ball or a player carrying the ball must touch the touch-line or the ground beyond it. A ball may be over the touch-line, and yet a player may still be able to catch it whilst his feet are in the field of play. If it has not landed, the ball is not in touch.

The ball can be kicked directly to touch from a penalty or if the kicker is in his own 22-metre area. Outside the 22-metre area, the ball must first bounce in the field of play or the throw is taken opposite where the kick was made.

The throw must be straight down the line of touch (an imaginary line at right-angles to the touch-line). There must be a metre gap between the two parallel lines of forwards. The gaps must be maintained until the ball is thrown. Until then players may

not hold, charge into or obstruct an opponent.

There must be a minimum of two players from each team in the lineout. The side throwing in decides the maximum number. The opposing team may have fewer lineout players but they must not have more. All players in the lineout must stand between the 5-metre and 15-metre lines. Players not taking part in the lineout must be 10 metres back from the line of touch.

The lineout begins when the ball leaves the thrower's hands. It ends when the ball leaves the lineout by being tapped back or being thrown over the 15-metre mark, or when a ruck or maul starts and moves beyond the line of touch.

Principles of Lineout Play

Forming of the Lineout

The two sets of forwards line up along the line of touch one metre from each other so that space is created between the two lineouts,

giving the players room and time to perform their roles.

The aim of the team throwing in the ball is to obtain controlled possession of the ball with which to go forwards, and provide a platform for the team to launch attacks, choosing from a range of options. If the opposition puts too much pressure on this control, it reduces the range of attacking options.

There are variations in the positioning of players. However, in selecting a team, two or maybe three players are selected primarily for their lineout catching ability. The tall catchers are traditionally positioned at 2, 4 and 6 in the lineout, with the other players at 1, 3 and 5, where they can support. In reality, this refers to the length of throw rather than the number of the person in the lineout. For example, in a three-man lineout a jumper can still be jumping at 6, in other words, 14–15 metres away from the throw.

The Jump and Catch

The side throwing in should try to create favourable mismatches when

Player position	Player number	Player role	Position in lineout
Hooker	2	Thrower	Front
Loose-head prop	1	Support	1
Tight-head prop	3	Support	3
Lock	4	Catcher	2 or 4
Lock	5	Catcher	2 or 4
Blind-side flanker	6	Support	5
No.8	8	Catcher	6
Openside flanker	7	Support of backs	7

forming the lineout. If one player is a better lineout forward than his opposite number, then a mismatch already exists. However, mismatches can also be created by changing the positioning and/or the numbers of forwards in the lineout or by plenty of movement of jumpers and lifters backwards and forwards in the line. The key player is the player who is going to jump and catch the ball. The catcher can draw the opponent away from the space into which the catcher wants to move. By dummying to go forwards and then moving back, space can be created behind the catcher; by dummying back and then moving forwards, space will be created in front. As the ball is thrown, this player should step to the centre before jumping to catch the ball. He is then able to jump vertically and is less likely to be pushed away from the ball when contact with his opposite number occurs.

The lock needs good body management in the air and hand dexterity. The lock should practise giving and taking passes above the head, using the fingertips; he also needs to be able to do this moving backwards and forwards, and when held up by supporters.

Supporting the Jumper

The support players on both sides of the catcher will support (lift) the catcher. The catcher should start the leap, and the support players will lift him to increase the height of the jump. The lifters take their timing off the jumper.

The Throw

As soon as the space has been created, the ball must be thrown accurately into it. The throw should be made down the line of touch so it is at catching height in the space into which the catcher has stepped when the player jumps and makes the catch.

Fig 105   Craig Gillies (Worcester Warriors) with support squeezing him high.

Distribution

The ball may be caught. However, there may be tactical advantages in deflecting it to another player in the lineout or to the scrum half. The deflection must be controlled.

Whilst the jumper is in the air, technically he cannot be tackled; however, a speedy return to earth will ensure a better front to the maul and a better drive with secured ball. The player should land in a semi-crouch position with his back to opposing players. This ensures a stable position, which will prevent opponents turning him.

If immediate delivery is not what is wanted, then players can form a maul once the ball has been controlled. The decision to deflect or pass the ball directly to the scrum half or to catch the ball and drive before delivery will depend on what the team perceives is the best option to achieve forward momentum.

Blocking and Driving

The remaining lineout players, with the exception of the tail-end player, should bind on each other to prevent the opposing players coming through and interfering with the ball and its distribution. If the ball is held in the lineout, players may group to use the driving option.

Summary of the Basics of Successful Lineout Play

• Communication: the pack leader or hooker gives a signal that decides the length of the line and another to indicate where the ball will be thrown. All lineout players should understand these signals.
• Variety: teams should have a range of lineout options, for example, the length of lineout (short or full); where the ball is to be thrown; how the ball is to be distributed (off the top, catch and give, catch and drive).
• Execution: the throw, the lift, the jump.
• Accurate throwing in.
• Agility: fast footwork to lose the opposition.
• Jumpers who have the ability to jump and to manage the body in the air.
• Effective support, from leaving until returning to earth.
• Balanced support so that supporters are at the top of their reach and applying equal forces from either side.

Getting the Technical Aspects Right

The Jump

Preliminary movements across the ground can lose the opposition jumper before leaving the ground. The jumper should start with his weight on the balls of the feet, knees bent, hands up and ready, head still, and eyes focusing on the ball. The jumper will have a range of sequences of quick steps, back or forward, followed by a gather and a jump. Examples of this are: feint one step backwards and go forwards one or two paces on to the front support player; feint one step forwards and go back one, two or three paces on to the rear support player. In the gather

Fig 106   Note the technical differences in the lift such as hand placements and the subsequent height of the jump.

KEY POINT

The jumper should step towards the line-of-touch so he is able to jump vertically. To gain maximum height from the jump, the jumper should drive up with both arms.

phase, the player bends at the knees, while maintaining an upright torso.

Whether going forwards or backwards, the jumper should also look to take a step into the middle of the line so that his actual jump is like a bound; that is, he jumps on to the take-off leg before driving explosively upwards. A dynamic jump is achieved by jumping off both feet. Hips, head, shoulders, arms and hands should be over the feet, and the legs should be bent at an optimum angle of 120 degrees.

The arms should assist the lift by swinging upwards but the elbows should be kept in and the arms bent. This speeds up the movement and gets arms up and away from obstruction. The jump should lead with the inside shoulder and inside leg (nearer the opposition). This helps the jumper turn his body slightly, giving greater protection of the ball, and enables him to land facing the scrum half.

The Lift

There are two lifters, one in front and one behind the jumper. Their role is to lift and support the jumper whilst he is in the air, and to bring him safely back to ground. Between them, they squeeze the jumper upwards so their support must be directly underneath him.

The lifters' movement across the ground and the lift must be synchronized. The lifters should concentrate on the jumper's feet or arms rather than watching the throw. A broad long step across into the gap should bring the prop's

shoulders parallel to the touch-line and facing his jumper. The lifter can now lift the jumper by locking the arms and driving with the legs into an upright position. The lifters should use the jumper's momentum, rather than trying to lift a dead weight.

A stable base is created by having both feet shoulder width apart, with knees bent and a flat back. Hands should be up and the arms bent with elbows tucked in. The eyes should be on the point of the intended grip: for the front lifter, this will be just above the knees on the thigh; for the back lifter, it will be where the thigh joins the buttock. This implies that the rear lifter will be taller than the front lifter, if the jumper is to be balanced in the air and both lifters extend their arms and legs and back to their maximum reach with locked elbows and knees. The power of the lift is delivered by their leg extension.

The Throw

The first precondition for the thrower is to prepare mentally by calming himself and refocusing. It is possible to do this by having a set routine for every throw. This might involve first talking to the scrum half to get the call, then going to the line and placing the toes on it, gripping the ball, focusing, and looking up.

Visualizing the flight of the ball to its target or a previous, successful performance, or concentrating on a single technical point will help in the execution of the skill. Self-talk can also be an aid, for example, 'This needs to be a high lob, landing on the 6,' for a lob to 4 going backwards.

The throw is two-handed. To avoid any pre-throw movement, which can act as a trigger for the opposition to attempt an interception, the thrower should hold the ball with both hands above the head, or further back behind the head, with the arms cocked ready to throw. This start position disguises the thrower's intention and also reduces

movement, which means there is less room for error.

The thrower responds to the movement in the line and the jump. As with the kick, everything should point in the direction of the throw and remain square: feet, knees, hips, chest, shoulders, arms and the ball. Any rotational activity will result in a throw that drifts off to the side. For right-handed throwers, the right foot tends to be forward on the line and pointing straight; the left foot is set slightly back. The weight is on the right foot and the knee is flexed to shift the weight forward.

The grip on the ball is an individual preference. The tendency is for right-handed players to use their dominant hand and grip the ball to the back and right side. The left hand supports and guides the ball and grips it to the front and left. There needs to be plenty of wrist action in the throw. The shoulders should stay square and the arms should continue to move in a straight line; this is done by turning the palms outwards with the thumbs pointing at the target. Spin on the ball is achieved by pulling the dominant throwing hand downwards. The ball moves across the palm and the fingertips.

The thrower needs to develop a variety of throws (which differ in terms of length, angle and speed) because of the number of permutations in the lineout, which can involve different jumpers, different parts of the lineout, and varying movement patterns in the jumpers.

STAR TIP

I try to work a lot on the timing of my jumps and I also need to work a lot with the hooker in training to tell him how I want the ball presented.
Olivier Roumat
(France)
(Rugby World)

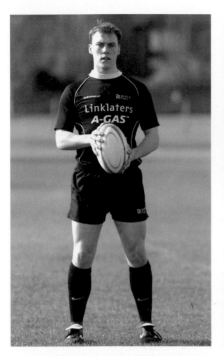

Fig 107   *The hooker composes himself. His body is square on the target, feet shoulder width apart.*

Fig 108   *Arms cocked, elbows in. No triggers given for the opposition.*

Fig 109   *From the side, knees bent.*

Fig 110   *The throw. Note body position remains square and hands follow through.*

Fig 111   *Completion of throw – side view.*

Most Common Throws/ Lineout Variations

Throwing to 2 jumper going forwards is probably the easiest ball to win. The throw is short and flat and less likely to be intercepted by the opposition. However, it is difficult to launch the threequarters from this possession, and setting up a drive is difficult because players have to come from the tail of the line to get into an effective driving position. There is also a danger of the maul being driven into touch by the opposition.

Throwing to 2 jumper going straight up allows the opposition the chance to intercept a throw that is too short or flat. The ball must be lobbed. This would only be attempted if the jumper is already dominating his opposite number.

Throwing to 4 jumper going forwards to land the ball between the opposition front jumper and their middle jumper means that the throw has to clear their 2 jumper and land short of their 4. It allows the opposition the chance to intercept the ball at 2, if the throw is too low.

Throwing to 4 jumper going straight up can only be achieved by taking the opposition by surprise and getting off the ground early. It would only be attempted if the jumping and lifting were well timed and the jumper had a height advantage over the opposition jumper.

Throwing to 4 jumper going backwards requires a lobbed trajectory and a long, accurate throw. Distributed off the top, it is a good ball with which to launch a back-line attack or a drive.

Throwing to 6 jumper going straight up can be risky because of the problem of accuracy of throw and clearing the opposition jumpers at 2 and 4. This is a particularly difficult throw in windy weather. It does engage the opposition back row, if caught and driven. Off the top, it is a good ball to launch a peel or give to the threequarters.

Play from Lineouts

The lineout would appear to be easier than the scrum as an attacking platform for the threequarters. The attacking threequarters are at least 20 metres from the defending threequarters. They have more time and space in which to operate. However, this extra space actually poses a few problems for the attackers.

For an attack launched through the threequarters, it is a long way to the gain-line. Most threequarter lines rarely reach it, if they move the ball to their wings. The defenders are not fixed; they drift out so that the last attacking player is confronted by two or three defenders. The tactical option employed by most teams, therefore, is to cross the gain-line near the tail of the lineout, perhaps by giving a flat ball to an inside centre or blind-side wing who is travelling fast and intending to crash through or into the defence. This player expects to be tackled. His job is done if the tackle takes place near the gain-line, and he can find his support players.

Where the Ball is Thrown

Quality possession for the threequarters depends on where the ball is thrown in the full lineout and the type of distribution given by the forwards to the scrum half. If the ball is thrown to 2, the fly half will have to stand closer to the tail of the lineout because of the length of the scrum-half pass. He will be closer, therefore, to the opposing open-side flanker. If the ball is won at 4, the fly half is a bit further from the opposing open-side flanker. If it is thrown to 6, the open-side flanker will probably be involved in the action, leaving the fly half with more time to take decisions.

Off-the-top deflection of the ball gives very quick service to the threequarters, but it means that the opposition back row can be flying out into midfield. Reasons for using this tactic would be to increase or maintain the tempo of the game; reduce the opposition's ability to react; initiate a sequence of play, for example, a front or back peel; or put a ball carrier over the gain-line quickly, perhaps a flat ball to the inside centre.

Caught and Given

If the jumper comes to ground before he releases the ball to the scrum half, the opposition back row gets held in, and this gives space and time for the backs to launch attacks. The lineout evolves into a contest between the attacking half-backs and defending back row, so the timing of the release of the ball should be varied to create uncertainty in the defence. The area at the tail of the lineout is key and has to be dominated. The further back the ball is thrown, the more options are opened up for the half-backs. It was once usual to have small open-side flankers because they would be quicker to the ball and more agile in snapping up loose ball. However, the increasing importance of the tail of the lineout, which provides the quickest way to cross the gain-line, means that tall players are needed in that area and open-side flankers now tend to be picked on their height.

Catch and Drive

A catch and drive sucks in the back row but allows the opposing threequarters to come up to the back foot of the maul and put pressure on the attacking threequarters. The opposition, however, has to work to stop the drive, and this can create space to attack elsewhere, particularly on the fringes. It can demoralize the opposition; put them on the back foot; tie them in; produce a good platform for the kicking game; allow the attacking team to cross gain line quickly. It is safer, and therefore is useful both in defence, and in attack.

Summary of Tactical Considerations

• Execute a move close in to a lineout when it has been driven.
• Backs strike out wide from ball off the top.
• Backs may have to adjust plans if anticipated lineout possession changes.
• The space to attack is created by the actions of the forwards.

Defensive Lineouts

What can be done when the opposition has the throw? There are three options to defend against an opposition lineout:

1. contest;
2. stand off;
3. drive.

Contest

• Anticipate where the ball will be thrown and try to intercept.
• Double lift – put jumpers up against 2 and 4 to compete in the air or disrupt the throw.

Stand Off

• Forwards quickly move to point of throw and react to any drive.
• Prepare for any peel.
• Be ready to move to the breakdown.

Defensive Drive

• The defending team can attempt to drive anywhere, but usually where there is a danger of an opposition catch and drive.
• Good body positions and leg drive are important.

Lineout Exercises

Practical lineout work falls into three main areas:

• Developing individual skills.
• Developing and co-ordinating sub-unit skills.
• Developing a unit strategy on own throw and opposition throw.

Individual Work

Throwing

For the thrower, there are a number of activities with a medicine ball that can help develop a fast arm, power and the general body mechanics needed for throwing:

• Using two hands, throw the ball into the floor as hard as possible, arching the body from toes to chest.
• Throw the ball backwards over the head, starting with the ball as low down as possible.
• Throw the ball from overhead position concentrating on a good arm, wrist, and finger extension.
• To develop fast arms and to use the lower back and hips, stand with arms overhead as if to throw; another player stands behind and grasps the thrower's wrists. Both pull against each other. Player behind releases the thrower and the thrower brings the arms through quickly to chase the throw.
• Shooting baskets: to develop a smooth, rhythmic throw and the idea of throwing from the toes, throw a basketball in the same way as a rugby ball. Concentrate on balance,

rhythm and arm action after throw.
• Throwing from the knees: to develop use of the lower back, the hooker sets up on his knees, , keeping the chest up. His partner stands 5 metres away with his hands on his head. He then raises his arms and presents his hands as a target, which the thrower aims to hit with a good 'snap'.
• Hitting a target (a goalpost): first, from 2 to 3m, repetitive throwing of • 10 to 20 balls in quick succession (fed by another player). This exercise should last 3–4 minutes. Progress backwards for the next 10 to 20 balls
• Throwing to the lineout to develop timing, reactions, speed and arc of different throws: first, the hooker works with pods of three (see below), practising different ball deliveries; next, do unopposed, semi-opposed or opposed drills using players in different positions as targets or opposition.

Movement, Jumping and Body Management

Two players face each other at a distance of 1.5 metres. Player A jumps and pushes the ball into the air for Player B. Player B jumps up and, whilst still in the air, catches the ball and returns it to Player A. Player A jumps and whilst still in the air catches the ball and returns it to Player B. The ball should be caught in two hands. The jumper should be at the top of the jump to take the ball.

In pairs: mirror image in movement back and forth and jump in 10-m zone.

One thrower plus two lineout players: one against one. 'Opposition' try to get in front of the jumper. The jumper tries to lose his opposition by moving up and down a channel. The throw is sent to the jumper when he is unmarked.

Hand–Eye Reaction Drills

• A player stands 1–2 metres from a wall, facing it. The coach stands

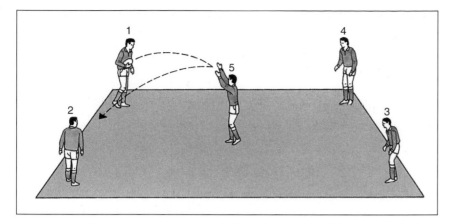

Fig 112 Jumping – exercise 2.

behind the player and throws a ball against the wall. The player must react and catch the ball or push it back on to the wall.

• Diagonal passing against a wall. Change the size and weight of the ball, and number the balls, so that players call out the number as well.

Sub-Unit Skills

Co-Ordination Practices For Lifters

Props face each other, palm against palm with knees bent. Eyes are focused on each other's knees. One leads and the other follows. The trigger for the lift is a sink at the knees. The one who follows replicates what his partner does in a mirror image and they lift together, finishing with chests almost touching. To progress this, forward or backward movement, and then both, are added, then the lift.

Tackle bags can be used as 'jumpers', with two supporters squeezing in on one bag. Fast arms are very important to get the 'jumper' up in the air quickly and the support must be underneath the jumper.

In pairs without a jumper, the lifters co-ordinate their movement over the ground, pause for balance and then drive dynamically upwards on the knee sink. One progression involves a pre-agreed sequence of steps, for example, go forwards 1 or 2 paces on to the front support player or go back 1, 2 or 3 paces on to the rear support player. Introduce fake movement, for example, forward then backward, and then lift.

Practices for the 'Pod' of Three

The jumper and his support start from static position. Two supporters assist the jumper up and hold him at arm's length for a count of 1-2-3. The objective is to develop a good support position, driving from the legs, hips in line with arms, and with a strong grip.

'Ping-pong': two pods of three work together to keep the ball in the air. Two jumpers with support face each other. Jumper A jumps up with ball and passes the ball to Jumper B, who has jumped and is being supported. Jumper A returns to ground and immediately jumps again to take a pass from Jumper B, who then returns to the ground and jumps again. The aim is to make five passes.

A pod of three working with four others in a square: the ball is fed to the jumper at the top of his jump and he then plays it 'off the top' or 'down and pop' to the next man in the square. The pod then sets up quickly and repeats the sequence on the new player with the ball.

Two pods of three and a thrower: no call is given, so the thrower has to respond to the movement sequence.

Lineout Games

For 'lineout end ball', there are two teams consisting each of a thrower and a jumper with two supporters. The winner is the first to get ten successful catches. The jumpers with their support move around to find space; the ball can only be thrown to them by the thrower once they are in the air. The ball is then placed on the ground and the pods move elsewhere. The thrower moves to the ball and throws again to the same jumper. If the ball is intercepted or dropped, it is turned over to the other team. The teams can then progress to attempting to get the ball over a try-line, a try being scored if one team catches the ball over the opposing goal-line.

CHAPTER 13

RESTARTS

Ten per cent of a team's primary possession comes from half-way kick-offs and 22-metre drop-outs. They represent an important supply of possession, and an appropriate amount of time in training should be devoted to practising restarts, both receiving and chasing. However, the onus is on the kicker to be accurate; if he feels he cannot be accurate, then it may be better to kick long and put the opposition under pressure by chasing effectively.

<table>
<tr><td>

LAWS CHECK

If the ball is kicked directly into touch from a kick-off, the non-offending team has three choices:

- kick again
- scrum at the centre
- lineout on the half-way

</td></tr>
</table>

Fig 113   Receiving kick-off: starting positions for the forwards.

Restarts from Half-Way

Receiving Kick-Offs

This is the positioning for a conventional reception of the kick. The majority of attacking restarts will be aimed to fall anywhere along the first line of receivers 7, 6, 5/3 and 4/1. Players 6 and 7 will be unsupported and isolated whilst jumping for the short, high kicks.

When receiving kick-offs, the catchers should leave plenty of space in front of them, into which they can run. They imagine themselves as 'goalkeepers' guarding their area. They need immediate support on either side.

Fig 114   Receiving kick-off: in the air.

The two locks are in a position to be supported by a lifter. The receiver of the ball is not allowed to be tackled whilst he is in the air, so the longer he is off the ground the more time he has to control the ball. The hooker can be the first support player to secure the ball should it be spilled.

No.6 must have the ability to receive a short kick himself whilst front of him. The second option, depending on the hang time of the kick, would be to pass long to 10 or 15, who would then put in a good clearing kick to touch.

Chasing the Kick-Off

A high kick gives time for the hunters to get under the ball and compete for it in the air. There should be two hunters who go after the ball and a predator who goes past the ball, looking for spilled ball. Generally, 5 and 8 will challenge for the ball in the air.

The chasing forwards must start their run from deep behind the half-way line on the kicker's hand signal. The fastest runner on the touch-line heads infield to intercept the kick or prevent the kick going directly to touch. If he starts wide, the ball can be seen for a longer time. The second wave of supporters seal off the ball, if it is caught, or tidy up any rebounds on their side. Frequently, the chasers palm the ball back.

One variation in the standard kick-off is to put in a deeper kick into the opposition 22 with as much hang time as possible, to allow chasers to apply maximum pressure. There are two lines of chasers: the back five in the scrum plus winger go up very quickly; and the front row forms a second wave. No.8 stays deep with the full back in case the opposition kick long.

A variety of kick-offs can catch the opposition off guard. One example is a split formation, with the forwards splitting into two pods of four players, one pod taking up a chasing formation on either side of the centre spot. The kicker then identifies the least-defended area and kicks accordingly. Another example involves the forwards lining up, but the restart kick going high and short, directly down the middle of the field. The primary chaser is a centre.

Fig 115 Receiving kick-off: the drive.

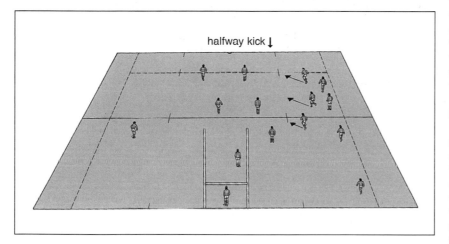

halfway kick ↓

Fig 116 Formation for receiving a kick-off.

unsupported, but he must also be ready to lift 5. No.3 must primarily stay with 5 but on longer kicks he must be able to react quickly and lift 4.

The scrum half can then pass to the No.8 charging into the midfield. There are a number of options after receiving the kick-off or drop-out and setting up a maul:

• attack the narrow side, the touch-line side, if there is sufficient room;

• attack the open side, if the kick is near the touch-line;
• kick long, down the tram-lines, deep into opposition territory, and chase.

If the kick-off has gone long and into the 22-metre area, the kick can be to touch.

For very deep restarts to 8 there are two options. First, 8 could simply crash the ball back up, trying to get as close as possible to his players in

22-Metre Drop-Outs

Receiving

The hooker and centre stand on the 22-metre line to cover the kicker taking a short kick to himself and also to charge down and exploit a poor drop-out. The larger of the two flankers (No.6) could be used rather than the hooker, because he will have greater height to charge down the kick.

The formation is very similar to that of a conventional half-way restart, with the receiving players covering as much space as possible. When receiving a 22 restart, it is very unlikely that the jumper will be lifted. The ball does not have to travel 10 metres as it does in a half-way restart, so the receivers have less time to react.

Chasing

The player taking the drop-out does not have to stand in the middle of the 22-metre line. The law allows him to take the kick anywhere along the line, and he should position himself about 10 to 15 metres to the right of the middle. He can then kick beyond the defending forwards because the ball is longer in the air having a longer distance to travel. The short drop-out to 6, 5 and 7 is high risk. It involves a short, hanging kick from 10 to allow chasers to exert maximum pressure and regain possession. Again, one player, perhaps 7, will go past the ball for the tap-back.

Variations

Get the ball quickly to the kicker and kick long. This forces the opposition to attack from deep. This kick must be followed up to prevent the opposition making ground. There are two waves of chasers: the first wave consists of the back row and the midfield backs and wingers, keeping together in a line spread across the field; the second wave consists of the front five and the scrum half filling in the gaps.

Another variation is for the kicker (open-side flanker) to tap it over the line to himself, and then pass it quickly back (through his legs) to the fly half, who starts a counter-attack or kicks it to touch.

PART 5
CONTINUITY

CHAPTER 14
CONTINUITY

Between the Set Pieces

Having won possession of set-piece ball, the object of any team is to move towards the opposition goal-line by running and passing, and by retaining possession when tackled. All players should be able to run evasively, pass accurately and retain the ball on contact with the opposition. Players should not regard themselves as forwards or threequarters; they have no number on their back between the set pieces.

Keeping the ball secure for five to six plays increases the chances of scoring because defences get pulled out of position. Rarely does a score come soon after a set piece because the defence tends to be well organized in such a situation. In order to play a fast-moving game, the ball must be produced and moved quickly away from the point of contact. The type of ball presentation depends on what has happened to the ball carrier in contact, and whether he has been brought to the ground or was able to stay on his feet.

Ball security depends on close support, communication and the ability to read the body language of the ball carrier. For the sake of continuity, it is better for the ball carrier to pass before contact and fix a defender by aiming at his inside shoulder. This prevents him drifting on to the receiver of the pass.

Passing before contact keeps the ball alive and makes it more difficult to defend.

If the ball carrier takes the ball into contact with the opposition, he is responsible for the ball; the support is responsible for dealing with the opposition. When tackled, the ball carrier has several options: pass (offload) in contact, or present the ball standing up and wait for support to come in and take it; pass through the tackle on the way to the ground or after hitting the ground; present the ball on the ground for the first support player to take decisions. The support player's options will be looked at later.

Passing Before Contact

The ball carrier should move the defender around by early passes or footwork (stepping right and passing to the left, for example). By aiming for the inside shoulder of the defender, he will fix him to the spot. The support player must shout either 'left' or 'right' so that the ball carrier knows where he is. They should act like a truck (ball carrier) and trailer (support player). As long as there is support behind the ball carrier, if the ball is dropped, it can be easily retrieved. The support runner can also see the opposition and go to the side that is undefended.

The support player should get on a running line just before receiving the ball, heading for gaps in the defence. To ensure he is coming from deep, he should be able to see the number on the back of the ball carrier before starting the run. Better to arrive late than early. He must accelerate on to the ball to get beyond the immediate defender and not over-run the ball and have to slow down. The pass must be flat. He then steps in towards the pass to straighten the line so that players can get outside.

Offloading in Contact

Often, a runner, having built up a head of steam, can take a pass from the scrum half close to a contact area and run into a defender. He will attempt to bump off the defender, but having lost momentum will try to pass to a support runner or hold on and present the ball for his support to come in and secure it. To do this, he needs to take a big power step with his shoulder, knee and foot in line. His body position before contact should be low, sinking the hips and bending the knees, with the chin up.

The ball carrier has to win the collision contest, and be in control of his body and the ball before considering the offload or presentation. When taking contact, the ball should be moved to the trailing shoulder. Adult, elite players can carry the ball into contact in a variety of ways because they have great skills and strength, and big hands. With young players, carrying the ball in the crook of the arm and on the chest, the short arm lever is probably the strongest carrying position.

Contact Skills

Fig 117 Groups of 3 up one channel and back along the next. Shield holders to oppose.

Fig 118 Ball carrier into contact: long last stride; hit with the side.

Fig 119 Give a gut pass; no daylight, the ball is put into the stomach of the receiver. Low body position for all.

depth and at pace. He transfers the ball with a short pass or sticks the ball into the stomach of the support player (a gut pass).

Offloading Through the Tackle

If the defender tackles low and around the hips, the carrier has the possibility of passing around his back to a support player. The ball carrier has to move the defender with some footwork to get him off his centre of gravity and force him to make an arm tackle rather than a shoulder tackle. The tackler drives at the hips of the ball carrier, who powers up and pushes his outside shoulder and hip through. He lifts the ball up and away from the body just prior to contact or brings the ball into his chest prior to bringing it off with both hands. He now makes the pass to his support player whilst sitting on the shoulder of the tackler, going around his back and gradually hitting the ground with knee, hip and shoulder.

Offloading After the Tackle

If the ball carrier's support is deeper than expected, or he is not sure that he is controlling the tackle, he can wait until he has hit the ground, and pass from there. The pass is two-handed and from the chest like a basketball pass.

Ball Presentation after the Tackle

When there is no immediate support or the ball carrier is not in control to give a pass, he should go to ground and present the ball. His presentation of the ball depends on the way he

He should aim for the edge of the defender to put the support player into the space behind the defender. The ball carrier 'opens the door' for the support player. For the centre of gravity to be over the legs, it is important not to lead with the shoulder. He takes a long last stride into contact for a wide foot base, which will help with balance.

After making contact with all his hard bits – hip and side – he should rock back so that his body weight is over both feet and he has a stable base. He is now in control to offload the ball to a runner coming from

Fig 120 Ball presentation on ground: ball an arm's length away; body at right angles to touch.

has fallen and the quality of the tackle. He has to release the ball immediately but should do so in a way that benefits his team and ensures possession is retained. The presentation is best done two-handed and reaching back as far as possible. The ball carrier will probably fall parallel to his own goal-line but should then jack-knife on the ground (he is allowed this second movement), using his core muscles to bring his torso around so that it is almost parallel to the touch-line. He can present the ball as close to his support and as far from the opposition as is feasible.

The reason for getting the ball away from the body is that it forces any opponent who tries to steal the ball into a weak position. If the tackled player holds the ball close to him, the opponent simply has to adopt a strong squat position, and he can lift the ball when he is very difficult to move. If, however, he places the ball well back, the opponent is stretching and is in a weak position and it is much easier to clean him out.

Support

If the ball is to be released before contact, the support player decides when by calling for it. In this situation, the support player must read the carrier's body language in order to understand his intentions. Is the ball carrier going to accept the contact? What type of tackle is it? Does he need to go in close (high tackle and arm movement is restricted) or can he keep some space between him and the ball carrier (low tackle and arms are free) for the pass?

After contact with the ball carrier standing, the first support player secures the ball. How? What actions should he take now? Hit, spin and pass? Hit, spin away and run for space? Hit and drive the original ball carrier?

After contact and the ball on the ground, the first support player has to decide where the ball is: his side of the breakdown or theirs? Does he lift the body out of the way first?

The general rule for a player at a ruck is to scan the situation and try to work out what his best contribution will be; he should not go blindly in just because the ruck is there. The first man to the tackle should go past the ball, unless it can be picked up, to get a body between the ball and the defenders.

His decision concerns the whereabouts of the opposition. Are they over the ball, or near it in numbers? Does the situation demand rapid clean-out getting below the would-be robber's body height to force him up and out, or can he pick and go or pick and pass? Those decisions are also influenced by the whereabouts of further support.

He has a number of tactical options: to go down on the ball, get up and offer; lift the ball and run; straddle the body, lift the ball and drive forwards; lift and pop to another support player; pick up and gut pass to support; pick up and offer (to create a maul); or drive over and leave the ball.

Support Play

Fig 121 Ball carrier with support either side and behind in the shape of an arrowhead.

Fig 122 After passing, provide support.

Fig 123 Keep the shape and the options available to the new ball carrier.

The First Support Player

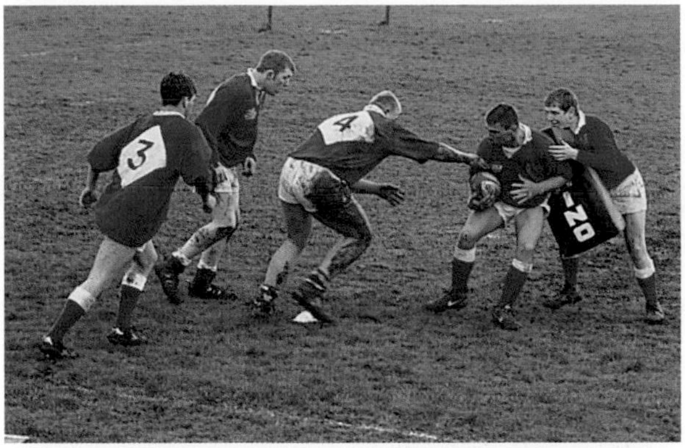

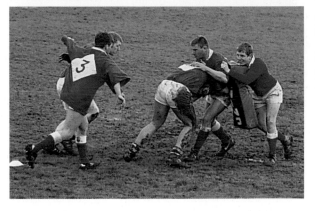

Fig 124 Ball carrier makes contact and turns all the way to face his support.

Fig 125 First support player goes in to secure the ball. He uses the first ball carrier as a battering ram.

KIT CHECK

When using tackle shields, hold the pad low to encourage low body positions and step back on impact to absorb the blow.

Ruck and Maul

Some argue that a breakdown is a failure to keep the ball moving. This is an over-simplification. A side may want to create a ruck or maul to disrupt the defence and suck in the opposition, taking numbers out of the defensive line. Whether the outcome of the initial ball carrier's contact with the defence is a ruck or maul depends on whether he stays on his feet to present the ball or ends up on the ground with the ball, and on what the support players decide.

According to the laws, 'A maul is formed by one or more players from each team on their feet and in physical contact closing around a player who has the ball' and 'A ruck is formed when the ball is on the

Ball Carrier in Contact

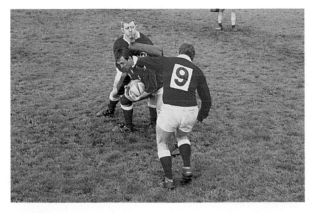

Fig 126 Support player secures by using outside shoulder to seal off the ball from the defender.

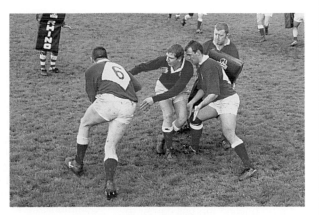

Fig 127 He spins and pops the ball to a third player in support.

ground and one or more players from each team are on their feet in physical contact, closing around the ball between them.'

There are a few advantages to the maul: it provides more options than a ruck; every player is on his feet and can get back into the game quickly; the off-side line is the back foot of the maul and this is constantly moving in rolling or driving mauls; and the defenders will be on their heels. If they are not dynamic, however, mauls slow down the game and allow the defence to reorganize. Under the laws of the game, if the ball gets wrapped up and does not come back, the side that took the ball into the maul loses possession.

The ruck tends to be more dynamic than the maul. The opposition are going backwards and this often allows the scrum half to move on to the ball, lift it and make a run himself, or pass an early ball to his threequarters. Rucks are better for the threequarters if the ball is delivered early, because they can see the ball and time their run better. The attacking threequarters will be on their toes and given more space.

Rucks are hit situations, which can upset the opposition and knock them out of their stride. To be effective for attacking purposes, rucks have to be quick so that the edges are still undefended. However, there is less control than a maul. The off-side line remains in the same place throughout so it is easier to defend. Teams commit few players to the ruck because they can see the ball is lost and that it will have to be passed, or the scrum half will have to run.

How to Maul

Mauling is a pair activity. The first support player isolates the ball by getting his hands on it. Other support players go beyond the ball carrier to isolate the ball further and protect the edges. The first player looks after the ball; the others look after the opposition.

When the ball carrier crashes into the defence, he must be able to distinguish between the contact and the breakdown point. If he makes contact with a defender, he must keep square and drive to make the breakdown point as far ahead of the contact point as possible.

When the drive ends, if the ball carrier has half-turned and a defender can get his hand and arm to the ball, the first support player should get hands on the ball and use the outside shoulder to seal off the ball, propping up the ball carrier with the shoulder under his chest. The next two players by-pass the first support player and ball carrier and take out the tackler. There should be balance; so one player goes left and one right. The body angles are in the rucking positions, spine in line and keeping the hips square. If a player finds himself with his back to the opposition after getting rid of the ball, he must work to face them and contribute to the drive. If he gets the ball to the back, it is protected and the end players can roll off.

Rolling mauls are normally executed on the opposition line, in an attempt to score, or to suck in players standing off the fringes of the maul. Transfer the ball to the back of the maul. Keep hips square and smuggle the ball back one-handed. The ball carrier presents the ball, the next player takes the ball with the same arm, in other words, if the ball carrier presents the ball in his right arm, the support player takes it in his right arm. This allows a rolling action to develop. He should be able to identify the moment when he needs to transfer control of the ball, when falling, or when someone wants greater control. Get bodies around the ball. Feel the wheel. Communicate to indicate the direction of wheel. Stay in contact. Block intruders. Keep it going.

How to Ruck

If the ball carrier is tackled to the ground, a support player 10 metres from the ball cannot do much. However, 2 metres from the ball a player is involved in the action. One metre and the player must appreciate what he has to do.

If the ball is on the ground and the opposition are closing, the first player should *bend*, and *drive* over the ball and clean out the opposition. He is not allowed to step more than a couple of paces beyond the ball because this is scatter rucking or obstruction. If the opposition are close, the first player could step over the body and the ball, bind on to the opposition, and wait for more support to drive them forwards.

The first player should hit the ruck with controlled speed and aggression. The key factors are to stay on your feet; keep opponents on their feet; get under and lift the opposition, with a low body, coming up; wide shoulders; pump legs with short strides and drive parallel to the touch-line; eyes open; go beyond the ball; head above shoulders; straight back with spine in line; chin up; keeping square.

Exercises

Contact Skills

The Fend

Using one arm, lean against a partner by placing a hand on his chest. Hold a ball in the other arm. Push away, then change arms.

Shoulder Dipping

One player holding a tackle shield and ball stands in the middle of a group of four, each numbered off. The coach calls a number and the nominated player drives at the pad holder. The pad holder dips and bounces off the would-be tackler.

Emphasize, hit and leave. The aim is not to spill the ball.

Truck and Trailer: First Support Player

Players are in large grids, in pairs with a ball. The ball carrier runs anywhere and the trailer must follow the ball carrier. No passes are made but they change roles on the whistle. Maintain the correct distance. Develop by giving gut passes to the trailer on the whistle.

Support of the Ball Carrier in Open Play

A group of five of six forwards in a narrow (10 × 30m) channel maintain bunched passing; they run up and down the channel, passing the ball to each other. Players call for the ball and the player on either side of the ball carrier provides him with passing options.

Change to close support passing to the left only, and then close support passing to the right only. Then change to one pass to the left followed by a pass to the right; then two passes left followed by one right; then pass to the inside player each time. The ball should not be transferred across the body. It is passed back in the direction from which it came in order to encourage straight running.

Each player is numbered. The ball carrier calls a number and the nominated player drives to the front to receive a pass. Now two numbers are called. The first nominated player receives a pass and gives the ball to the second nominated player.

Make one player a defender. The defender must keep the ball in front of him and try to stop the pack from getting the ball to the end of the channel. Use more defenders. Place defenders along the channel and bring each defender in from different angles. Two defenders run along with the group, being a nuisance and getting in the way.

Committing the Defender

In fours or fives the first ball carrier runs 5 metres, puts down the ball, runs on a few more metres, turns and opposes. The second player retrieves the ball, fixes the defender by running at him before passing and putting a second support player into space. The cycle starts all over again.

Now the first player tackles low. The ball carrier passes out of the tackle.

Then the tackle is high, and the third player drives in and spins off; or he drives in and feeds the fourth player.

Driving Position

Exercise 1

Four players are in a line, holding on to the shorts of the player in front. A ball carrier is to try and touch the tail-end player with the ball. This drill is good for developing low running. Bend knees, sink hips, and keep head up. Maintain a wide stance and a strong grip on the ball, which is held in two hands.

Exercise 2

Players work in fours, one of whom is a pad holder. The three take it in turns to sink the knees and drive the shield backwards over a short distance.

When they are preparing to drive into contact, they should hunch the shoulders, and tense the muscles of the neck, chest and shoulders. They should also breathe in and hold their breath. This will solidify the upper trunk. The chin is kept off the chest, and the eyes look 'through the eyebrows; at the intended target. The back must be kept straight, or slightly hollowed, with the shoulders above the hips.

Ball Presentation off the Ground

Exercise 1

The coach walks between two lines of players who are facing each other and paired off. The coach gives the ball to one player. The ball carrier drives into his partner and presents the ball again for the coach who gives it to another pair. Move the pairs closer to increase pressure. Rotate the players to give variety of opponent.

Exercise 2

In sixes – three on the 5-m line and three on the 15-m line (Fig 128) – one runs, picks up the ball (which is 2 metres out) and places the ball 2 metres out opposite the second player who runs out and lifts the ball and places it for the third player to pick up.

Progressions of this drill are:

- Player 1 picks up, runs, plants the feet, checks side on and gives the ball to Player 2 coming from the opposite direction.
- Players 1 and 3 go together – 1 runs and plants feet and pops the ball to 3 who plants his feet and gives a gut pass to 2 who plants his feet and gives a pop pass to 4 (Fig 129). 4 plants his feet and gives a gut pass to 5, who plants his feet and gives a pop pass to 6.
- Change to working in pairs. 1 runs, plants feet and gives a gut pass to 2, then loops outside to be given a pop pass. He hands on to the next pair.
- Player 1 runs, stops, turns; 2 takes and rolls off, runs on and back, stops half-way and 3 comes in and takes (Fig 130).
- Allow 5 seconds struggling with ball before release; drive through, hips stable, and sway outwards.
- Run with head up, rip ball and pop up to third player who runs on and brings ball back to the middle for the next player to come in and rip. Support runner arrives late and fast.

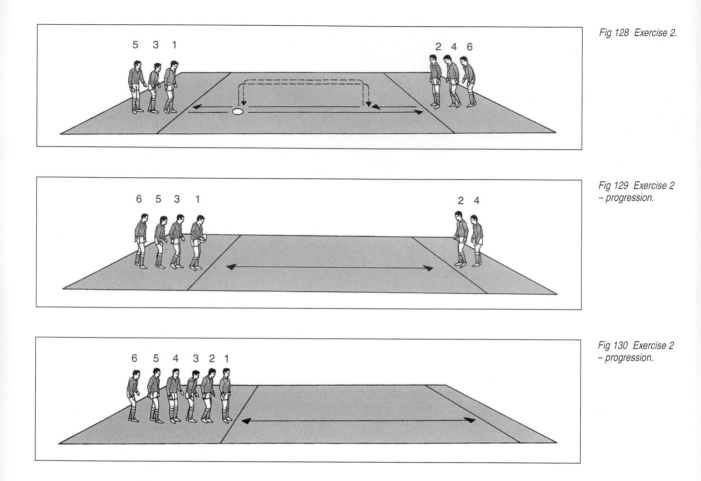

Fig 128 Exercise 2.

Fig 129 Exercise 2 – progression.

Fig 130 Exercise 2 – progression.

Passing in Contact

Fig 131 Ball carrier into contact: long last stride and unbalance the defender.

Fig 132 Ball carrier gives soft, flat pass to support player who adopts a low body position and calls for the ball.

- Ripper passes ball to opposite side so he rips and half-turns.
- Add two support runners.

Offloading in the Tackle

Two staggered lines of pad holders keep their pads low to encourage low running. Go in pairs, with a ball carrier and a support player. 1 passes to 2 who drives into the first pad. He passes out of the tackle to 1 who returns the pass to 2, who drives into the next pad. On the return route, 1 drives and 2 keeps passing the ball back to him. Use alternate shoulders and vary the way the ball is presented. The pressure is increased by bringing the pads closer together.

Offloading through the Tackle

In a channel over 15 metres wide two defenders are on their knees with their arms out. There are three attacking players. Real tackles are applied by kneeling defenders. Ball carriers distribute the ball behind the back of the defender and on the way down.

Ball Presentation after the Tackle

Exercise 1

Picking up the ball with a body in the way: one ball for six players grouped in threes. Each group, 5 metres apart, in single file and facing each other. Ball carrier runs, falls, rolls and plants the ball close or long. Player from opposite group steps over the body, lifts the ball, rolls and plants the ball, and the sequence continues.

Exercise 2

Five players start in single file. First player runs 5 metres, falls to the ground and presents the ball. The next player straddles him and picks up the ball. The sequence continues over 40 metres.

Distribution in the Tackle

Fig 133 Line of defenders on knees, ball carrier takes ball into contact.

Fig 134 He passes around the back of defender. Give sufficient time in the air for the support player to take the ball.

A progression is for the support player to keep his position and give a gut pass to another support player who also steps over the body on the way.

Clearing-Out Exercises

Ball Presentation on and off the Ground

In threes, the ball carrier drives into a shield holder and goes to ground, placing the ball. A support player cleans out the shield holder. Player 3 lifts the ball, then they jog back to the start position and change roles.

Now regroup in fives with one shield holder. The ball carrier drives in, turns and presents the ball. Player 2 strips the ball; 3 and 4 cross bind and slip over 2 on to 1; then 2 goes to ground.

Pick Up and Pass: Running Angles

Exercise 1

The ball is on the ground at X (Fig 135), with 1 and 2 running from a

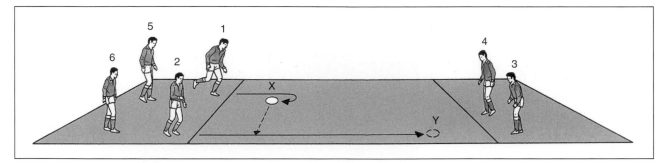

Fig 135 Pick up and pass – Exercise 1.

start line. Player 1 steps beyond the ball and lifts it, and 2 shouts 'wide' or 'close', 'left' or 'right'. Player 2 places ball at Y for the next two to go.

Now 2 angles back behind the breakdown point, where the space is. Then 2 starts behind 1 and arcs out and gets on a straight running line before receiving the ball. Progress by adding defenders at X and Y. Player 1 runs at opposition at X, passes before contact, passes in contact, drives in for 2 to rip and roll. Player 2 repeats this on Y so 1 has to recover quickly to support.

Exercise 2

Use three tackle bags on their sides (Fig 136). A ball is placed near the end of each bag at alternate ends. A ball carrier runs to the first ball, places his ball and picks up the ball already there. He passes wide to a support player who runs on and places his ball next to the second ball. He picks that one up and passes wide to the first ball carrier who runs on and places the ball next to the third ball. He picks that ball up and passes wide to his partner.

In a development of this routine the support player has to take a short pass near the end of the bag where the ball is. He will have to arc around to get on the correct side (Fig 137). Now let the support

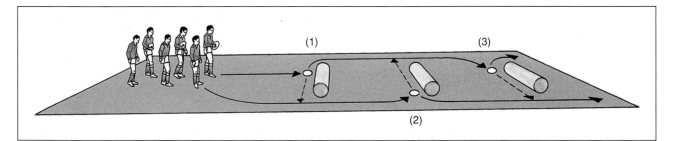

Fig 136 Exercise 2.

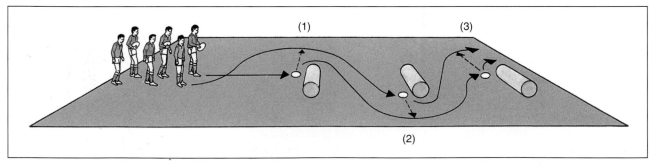

Fig 137 Exercise 3.

Fig 138 Contact pad work – exercise 4.

player choose, making sure that he communicates with the distributor.

Collective Support

Players work in fives against a tackle shield holder. Player 4 hands on the ball and seals off the ball. Two support players take out the defender with inner arms slipping over the ball carriers. An early ball is played to an acting scrum half.

Decision-Making

A group is to progress along a channel 10 to 15 metres wide, the length of the field (Fig 138). They are opposed by an equal number of shield holders. Running at half pace, the attackers must run at the gaps in the defence, take decisions when to pass, whether to take the ball into contact and how to present the ball (off or on the ground). The defenders keep getting back between the ball and their own line.

Lifting the Ball

Fig 139 Step beyond the ball, straddle the body to protect the space beyond the ball and be in a strong position.

Fig 140 Bend the knees, sink the hips, lift the ball.

Fig 141 And go!

Fig 142 Straddle, lift.

Fig 143 Gut pass to support player to maintain momentum. The support player also steps over the body.

CHAPTER 15

DEFENCE AT THE BREAKDOWN

The Importance of Defence

Defence wins games. A team of tacklers cannot be beaten. During a game, a team is called upon to make anything between 60 and 130 tackles. If a team's effective tackle rate is lower than 75 per cent, it will lose. A great tackle that turns over the ball, and gives a team an opportunity to launch a counter-attack, can also win games. Considering that half the match time is played without the ball, a team's defensive patterns and tackling have to be practised in training. To be effective in defence, the team has to dominate the opposition physically, go to meet the attack and gain ground; it has to apply pressure to the passing line and turn over ball through offensive tackling.

Organization of Defence

The successful defence will be organized and each player will be technically proficient in the tackle. The aim is to spread a defensive line across the field. The defence moves forwards and across. The forward

movement cuts down the space and time the attackers have and prevents the defensive line being outflanked. If the defenders place their outside foot forward, their first steps will be forwards.

The defence should work in threes: one on the inside and one on the outside of the man intending to tackle the ball carrier. If the ball carrier tries to go on the outside or step back inside, the space is covered, as are loops and switches. All players must keep in line with each other and on the inside of their immediate opponent.

Statistically there are more rucks and mauls than there are scrums and lineouts, and it is from these secondary phases that most sides are looking for gaps in the defence. Defences must be well organized from phase plays. A defence should not commit too many players to the ruck or maul, if it is a lost cause.

By doing this, the defence will have the advantage of numbers because the attack will commit players to securing possession. The defence should work together as a line, not as individuals.

As the defence moves into position, the players should be numbering up the attacking players on either side of the ruck or maul in case the attack has the advantage of numbers on one side. The scrum half should be commanding this and telling the players where they are needed.

The line should extend at each side of the ruck. Who goes where is determined by the arrival times of players. As a guide, the bigger the player, the closer to the fringe, because this is where attacking sides

will put their big running forwards. The defence needs big men to tackle them. Generally, the back row will be involved in the contact area, and it will be the props and locks who arrive next and take up these positions on the fringes. As the ball is moved further from the breakdown area, the quicker players will fill in the outside spaces.

The defence should move up simultaneously at either side of the ruck. Defenders drift across after the ball once it has passed them. They should not leave their line after the ball has passed them; they need to remain in place to cover any switch-back by the attack.

At the edge of the breakdown, a defender (guard) positions himself on the inside shoulder of the first defender. The guard does not mark anyone; he protects the inside shoulder channel. If the attacking scrum half runs across, the first defender can go up to tackle him, knowing that the guard will take any runner who comes back on the switch. All the players go up but the guard is less dynamic because of his protective role. The scrum half gets behind the breakdown to cover anyone coming through the middle,

---

LAWS CHECK

A player joining a ruck or maul must do so from behind the hindmost player of his own team.

KEY POINT

Do not allow the maul to become static before giving the ball back, as this allows the defence to reorganize. Keep the maul dynamic and then present the ball. If it becomes static, forwards must redrive before delivery.

and he controls the defence, then acts as a sweeper behind the defensive line.

Communication

Communication is vital for a successful defence. The scrum half is the linch-pin, but all defenders must be talking. The key talk comes from the inside. Players should talk to one another about whom they are marking, about the numbers situation at the breakdown and about the speed at which the line moves up.

The Rush Defence

There has been a shift in the game from the 'in-and-out' defence to the 'up-and-in' or 'rush' defence. One-on-one tackles are still essential. However, the rush involves the defender standing on the outside of his man and coming up fast to make a tackle on his inside shoulder. The outside-in defence depends on line speed and is a very aggressive defence because the defender attacks the ball carrier from the outside and on his blind side, when his eyes are on the ball. However, it is vulnerable. Due to the speed of the line, defenders on the outside can sometimes get ahead of slower inside defenders, thus enabling the ball carrier to see the space and head for the gap. This defence relies on the wing hitting in on the ball carrier – that is, being ahead of his insides – so it can also be vulnerable to the chip or grubber since there is always space behind – a diagonal kick or grubber. There are a number of ways of beating it: going through the line with switches, show and goes after holding with decoy runners, a wide pass and an inside pass. Decoy runners can confuse and isolate defenders because the line is moving so quickly there is little time to react.

Fig 144 Alex Brown (Gloucester) unable to resist Worcester's driving maul.

Exercises

In-and-Out Defence

Drill 1

Four defenders begin unopposed on the coach's signal to practise moving together and communicating when to move in. Four defenders (D) now work in sets of five hits against four bags (X). Work both 'out to in' and 'in to out'.

Watch the ball and scan the opposition. As a progression, the whole group of players move to their match positions by running arcs (Fig 145).

Drill 2

Four defenders defend against three bag holders in a line and one bag arriving late as a strike runner. Defenders have to pick the extra man, to make their hits (Fig 146). They need

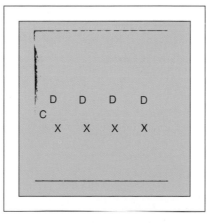

Fig 145 Four defenders against shield holders.

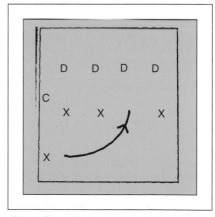

Fig 146 Four defenders against a strike runner coming into the line.

to work together, communicate, scan the ball and their opponents, defend either 'in to out' or 'out to in', and ensure correct shoulder at contact.

Drill 3

Two defenders oppose five attackers putting pressure on handling and working as a pair. Two defenders move backwards and forwards together between the cones. The coach feeds the ball to the five attackers who are 5 metres away (Fig 147). The attackers try and beat the advancing defenders who come up and out together in an attempt to get to the outside man. They should stay inside and tight, go up and sideways without getting too square.

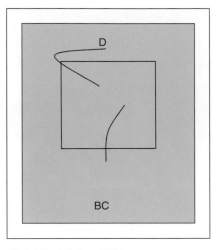

Fig 148 Rush Defence Drill 1.

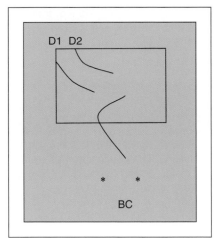

Fig 149 Rush Defence Drill 2.

point of contact, gets his feet close to push off and approaches from the inside with the inside shoulder

Drill 2

Two defenders against one attacker. D1 works on the inside shoulder; D2 adjusts on the outside shoulder. He gets square and slightly behind D1, forcing the ball carrier between them. Now the outside goes up in front as in the rush (Fig 149).

Drill 3

Defender D2 covers the SH. There are three defenders on the inside of the attacking fly half. D4 is on the outside of the fly half. The scrum half to go if D2 wide – dummy and go; if D2 stays, he gives an inside pass to a support forward (back flick) (Fig 150).

As a development, the fly half can stand wider to pull the defence wider and create gaps for an inside pass to the blind-side wing.

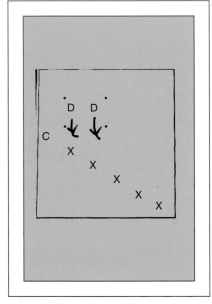

Fig 147 Up-and-out defence drill.

Rush Defence

Drill 1

Tracking and footwork by the defender are involved in this drill. The defender touches the corner cone, and the ball carrier goes, his intention being to get to the line opposite. The defender squares up his shoulders at

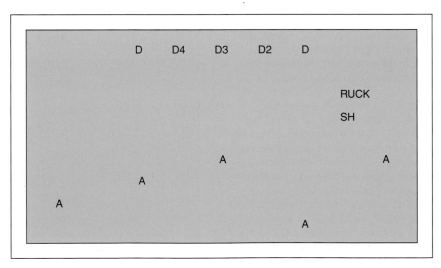

Fig 150 Rush Defence Drill 3.

Fig 151 Exercise: Driving maul: moving the ball to the back with one arm. Face the front, spine in line and hips square.

Driving Maul

Fig 152 Ball carrier turns, first player secures the ball and drives on the original ball carrier. Support players cross bind and drive on him.

Fig 153 Progression: forwards converging and binding.

Fig 154 A driving maul: the ball is smuggled to the back of the maul.

PART 6

THE THREEQUARTERS

CHAPTER 16
THREEQUARTER PLAY

Coaching the Threequarters

The vast majority of coaches see their players twice a week. Generally, the first session gets divided between the warm-up, skill enhancement and contact work, and then the backs and forwards divide to practise their unit skills. The second session's emphasis is generally on unit and teamwork. In either session the backs have the opportunity to work together. What do you want to achieve?

The session with the backs should rarely last longer than 45 minutes. The backs tend to run around in training more than the forwards, whose sessions usually revolve around scrum and lineout. If the session is planned well and there is a fitness component in the intensity of the session, then the 45 minutes will be enough.

It is also advisable to distinguish between a coaching session and a training session. A coaching session tends to be of a low-level intensity, with much emphasis on organization (practice of moves, for example). A training session is when you have large numbers and inclement weather, and it is important to cover fitness and skills, and drill the players. A good session has a mixture of coaching and training.

In terms of coaching behaviours, what the coach says should be kept to a minimum. Words should be carefully chosen; he should be concise and not long-winded; he needs to bring out the key principles, the main coaching points (and do this gradually, not all at once).

Sometimes, coaching may not be necessary because everything is going well; in this case, a few points should be raised to say what is going well. Whether the coach uses a question-and-answer technique or explains to the players without involving them depends on his personality, the time available and the weather conditions. It is all circumstantial and coaches should develop their own style – provided it is successful and the players enjoy it!

What should be covered in those sessions? When conducting a practice session with threequarters, a coach should observe the following:

• Build each session from simple to complex; from technique to skill; from individual to unit.
• Vary the defence: where they are coming from, their numbers, and the speed of approach. Make the backs operate under pressure.
• Vary the quality of the ball. In match situations how often does the midfield get the perfect ball?

Individual skills are at the heart of threequarter play. If they are not mastered, then it is impossible to use the threequarter unit and a team's options are restricted. It is impossible to cover every skill in each session. It is important, however, to have a checklist of skills and to prioritize them. Each back line has different qualities and skills levels. What works for one line may not work for another.

Checklist of Threequarters' Skills

• Passing: how to pass and receive; where to pass; what type of pass to use; when to pass – how far from the opposition?
• Running lines: different angles of run to create an advantage; switches and loops.
• Running speeds: controlled running; evasion; the line moving at different times and speeds.
• Alignment: passing line: starting positions; timing of run; relationship of gain and tackle lines; self-knowledge; understanding of defensive organization.
• Decision-making: simple decisions – two against one; complex decisions – four against three; awareness of space, time and numbers; risk or gamble?
• Contact: off the ground; on the ground; continuity.
• Attacking ploys: purpose; functional roles.
• Counter-attack: where from? Principles or patterns? Who decides?
• Kicking: type of kick; where from and to where? Why?
• Defensive organization: what system? When? Who tackles which opposing player?

Passing

Threequarters need to develop the ability to pass flat with confidence whilst running at the defence when it is close. They also need to be able to pass at varying lengths, from a short, soft pass held briefly in the air for a close runner to a long ball discharged at a distant space for a straight or angled runner. They must pass sympathetically to suit the situation.

When to pass means involving the opposition and good decision-making. How far from the opposition do you make your passes? When it is two against one, the first ball carrier must not get too close so he gets caught with the ball; and he must not pass too early so that the defender can move out and tackle the last player. If the receiver does not need to pass, pass in front of him, into space for him to run on to.

If it is three against two, the first ball carrier must not pass too early so the defenders are allowed to drift out and the situation becomes two against two. Neither should he pass too late, so that the middle player gets man and ball. The pass must be to the receiver's hands and the receiver will reach out to take the ball early.

KEY POINT

Give passes far enough away to fix the defender but allow time for the next carrier of the ball to get his pass away.

Running Lines

How do you stop a defender drifting out to tackle the player you have just passed to? How do you interest him enough to take him out of play without playing yourself out of the game (unless there is a two against one to score)? The timing of the pass is important, as is the running angle of the ball carrier.

What line does a player run? Does he attack the inside or outside shoulder of the defender? Angle back at cross-cover defenders or run away from them towards the touch-line? Much depends on intentions. If it is two against one, aim at the inside shoulder of the defender to

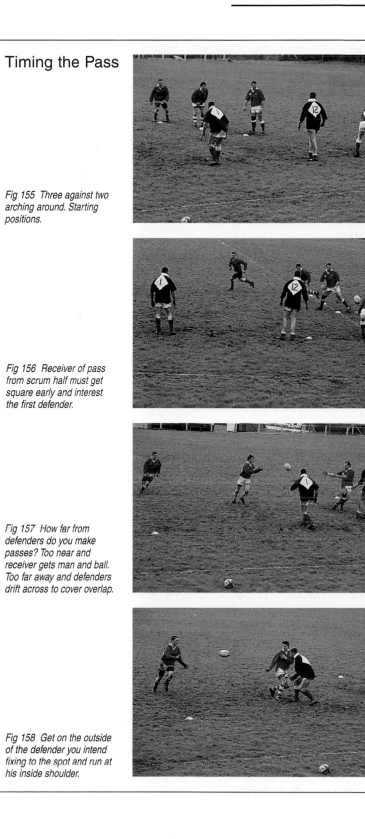

Timing the Pass

Fig 155 Three against two arching around. Starting positions.

Fig 156 Receiver of pass from scrum half must get square early and interest the first defender.

Fig 157 How far from defenders do you make passes? Too near and receiver gets man and ball. Too far away and defenders drift across to cover overlap.

Fig 158 Get on the outside of the defender you intend fixing to the spot and run at his inside shoulder.

prevent him drifting out. Try to get on the outside of a defender to attack his inside, if you aim to pass out. If the cross cover is to be taken out, and the space on the outside kept available for support runners, run back at the defenders.

Running Speeds

Discipline and confidence are needed to run at 75 per cent speed to remain in total running control, with the opportunity to change line or pace if required to evade a defender. This allows a player to retain the capacity to pass the ball close, pass the ball wide, kick, play the ball off early, or hit the tackle and present the ball.

Alignment

A back division needs to play on top of the defence. This will mean that the passing is flat to keep each individual defender interested in his man or zone. It does not, however, mean that the starting alignment has to be flat. For example, if the backs wish to inject pace for a strike attack then this will not come from a player who standing flat and close to the defence when he starts his run. Each threequarter does not have to start to run at the same time nor move at the same speed.

The first attack may be a skirmish to disorganize the defence and the real strike is intended to come later. In this case, other factors become important, including control of the ball, running lines, running speeds and targeting opposition players.

What considerations are taken into account in deciding on the depth of the threequarters' alignment? The attacking line must be aware of its own ability in running, pace and agility, handling, confidence, the strike point of the attack, and general attacking strategy (attack a thin defence, move the ball from congested areas so that penetration can take place). Do the backs understand the importance and relationships of the gain- and the tackle lines? Do they understand the organization of the defenders and the speed of their approach?

When do they run? Do they all start together? Does each threequarter delay his run until the inside player has the ball in his hands? Where do the blind-side wing, the open-side wing and full back stand at lineouts or scrums?

There is no one way to align. The important factors are *time* and *space* and *intentions*, for example, whether the fly half wants to interest the No.7 or intends to move the ball quickly. Alignment is established on the players' speed of hand and the number of passes to the play maker. The strike runner must have his requirements considered: does he want late or early ball?

Decision-Making

Simple decisions are to be taken in small practices, for example, 2 v 1, 3 v 2, when you are asking players to decide when to pass and fix defenders. More complex decisions which are game-oriented, for example, counter-attacking situations, should also be practised. Consider the decisions that have to be taken at second- and third-phase possession. Do the half-backs have their head up and eyes open? Is the numbers game to your advantage? Where is the space to attack? Does the attack have support? Play with ball pinched from the opposition so the attacking line is receiving ball going backwards.

Deal with the cross-cover defence after a breakthrough. These defenders are coming across the field at angles that are different from those used in the first line of defence.

Contact with the Defence

All threequarters must be able to control the ball in contact, both on the feet and on the ground. Pressurizing defenders means accepting pressure, and contact is inevitable. The ball must be kept alive.

Backs must support each other. If the ball has been moved wide then it is difficult for forwards to get to the contact area. The threequarters must be able to maul and ruck as well as the forwards, because there may be no forward about. Pass and support. The primary support gets behind the ball carrier. If a threequarter is outside the ball carrier, who is caught in possession, he should stay there.

Attacking Ploys

The success of a move depends on quality ball from the forwards and attacking organization to vary the point of attack. Decoys commit the defence and disguise the main strike area. Alternatives to each move can also be developed by having the capability of actually using the decoy runners as the main strike. Provide immediate support of the breakthrough.

What is the purpose of the move – to disorganize an organized defence and then attack the spaces, or to achieve a breakthrough and score from first-phase possession? In which part of the field should a particular ploy be used? Some moves work better off the right-hand side of the field; some are better when the primary possession is from a lineout rather than a scrum.

Scrum ball offers a number of attacking advantages:

- good-quality ball is usually delivered unless the scrum is going backwards;
- the opposition forwards are crammed into a narrow channel;
- the defending backs normally use a man-for-man defence;
- there are left and right options available;
- the defenders are close, thus reducing their reaction time; and
- the position of blind-side wing is very difficult.

There are some attacking disadvantages associated with lineout ball:

- quality ball is unreliable;
- the forwards are in a wide channel;
- the defending backs can use a variety of defences;
- left or right options only are available; and
- the opposition is 20 metres away and has plenty of reaction time.

Counter-Attack

Are you prepared to counter-attack? Are you prepared to take risks? A two against one is a risk; a one against two is a gamble. From which areas of the field are you prepared to counter-attack – the whole width of the field or just inside the 15-metre channels, with the greater possibility of getting the ball to touch, if things go wrong?

Who decides that a counter-attack is on – the receiver of the ball or a support player? The receiver is concentrating on the ball and does not have the peripheral vision of the support player. However, if the receiver catches the ball cleanly and running at full speed, does he really need someone else to decide whether he should counter-attack or not?

Does the counter-attack operate in set patterns? If the ball is caught by the blind-side wing, does he pass

long inside to the full back and then run in support? If the ball is taken by the full back does he do a switch with the blind-side wing? If the kick goes to the open-side wing, does he do a switch with the full back? Or does the counter-attack understand and remain guided by general principles? Dummy to strength, take the ball into space.

A Kicking Strategy

What type of kick should you use – the bomb, punt, drop kick, chip, or grubber? And why – to find the safety of touch; to chase and recover possession; or to turn a defence? The bomb, for example, is used by the fly half with designated chasers, one to compete for the ball in the air and the other to snap up loose ball. The aim is to recover possession, going forwards and behind the front line of defence.

Defensive Organization Systems

Man-for-Man

The threequarters mark their opposite numbers. This is generally in second-phase situations. The midfield players come up staggered, 1 metre behind the inside player. The gain-line is sacrificed because the centres are further back. However, there is a better chance of watching the opposition, making tackles and not getting caught flat so that the ball carrier can take the tackle, and pass around the back of the tackler to a close support runner.

Drift

Initially, the threequarters stand marking their opposite number. When the ball comes out, if the opposition fly half passes immediately, the defenders slide across to mark the man outside their opposite number. For example, the fly half takes the inside centre and the inside centre takes the outside centre.

One-Out

The defenders stand one out from their opposite numbers, usually at lineouts. With both drift and one-out, the open-side wing forward must mark the fly half who has been left unmarked by the defending fly half.

Overlap

If the full back enters the line, the open-side wing moves in to mark him. This leaves an overlap situation if the full back gets the pass away to his wing. The defending full back takes the last man. This is generally used inside the defending 22-metre area.

Isolation

From scrums, if the full back enters the line, wings stay on wings and the other defenders turn and isolate the ball carrier so he has no one to pass to. The defending full back has to tackle him.

Crescent/Umbrella or Rush

This involves the defender standing on the outside of his man and coming up hard to make a tackle on his inside shoulder (the traditional way is to be on the inside and push out to take the attacker on your outside shoulder). The outside-in defence depends on line speed and is a very aggressive method of defence because you attack the ball carrier from the outside and on his blind side, when his eyes are on the ball and not on you.

Drills for Threequarters

Passing

Each group of four take it in turns to cross the grid (Fig 158). One ball is needed; the first wave runs across the grid and passes along the line to the end man. He passes on to the group waiting. The ball is passed to the end man who gives it to the next wave.

This exercise can be developed in a few ways:

• On a signal from the coach, the ball carrier simulates a tackle and holds the ball up. The person who passed goes in and rips, and passes to a player who is looping.
• Add two shield holders and a scrum half (Fig 160). The fly half takes a flat pass from the scrum half and gets the pass away under pressure. So does the next attacker. When do the outside men run, if they are to inject pace? When Line 1 has gone through, the scrum half and defenders move across to the other side of the grid to defend against Line 2.
• Make the two defenders mark the two middle attackers.
• Include a defending back row to cover across behind shield holders.

Running Lines

Arrange a group of four against three in a narrow channel (Fig 161). Players B, C and D run at the same time as A runs; A passes to B, B to C, and C to D. Fix the defenders to create the overlap.

Develop this drill with the scrum half and group of four backs jogging up the field, staying between touch and the 15-metre line. They are opposed by two defenders and have to stop them drifting (Fig 162). When the ball gets to the end, the backs realign and go again. Keeping to a jogging pace throughout, they prevent the drift by attacking the

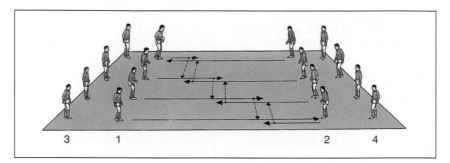

Fig 159 Passing.

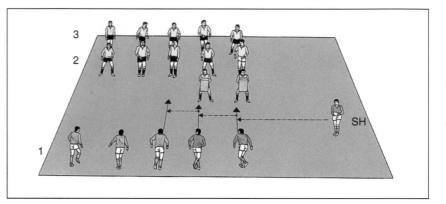

Fig 160 Passing (progression).

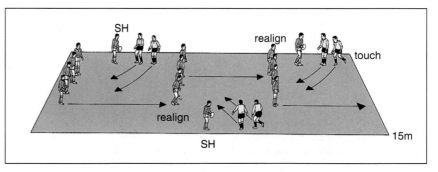

Fig 161 Running lines.

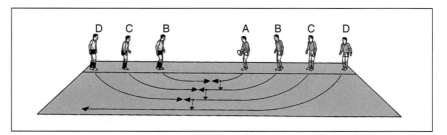

Fig 162 Running lines (progression).

inside shoulder of the defender; doing dummy switches; and passing back inside and then out again.

Realignment

Players work in groups of five running along a narrow channel and passing. When the ball gets to the end player, he runs off at an acute angle, stops and acts as a scrum half as the rest realign on him. He then passes the ball and the procedure is repeated.

Creating Space

To practise drawing the cross cover to the outside and passing inside, players work in threes down a channel, with defenders stationed at regular intervals (Fig 163). They are to be drawn to the outside by a change of running direction by the ball carrier, who then passes inside to support.

Counter-Attack

In fours, one player acts as a defender. The drill starts on the goal-line, the coach rolls the ball 10 metres, three attackers get back, one falls and pops up the ball. The two remaining attackers beat the defender, who now comes into the action. They have to return the ball to the goal-line.

Develop the drill by placing players in waves of threes about 10 metres from the coach. The coach kicks a ball to each wave in turn and they are to counter-attack in set patterns. They are acting as the full back and two wings. If the full back receives the kick, he switches with the blind-side wing who links with the open-side wing. If the open-side wing receives the kick, he dummy switches with the full back and switches with the blind-side wing. If the ball goes to the blind-side wing, he gives a long pass to the full back who runs towards the coach but

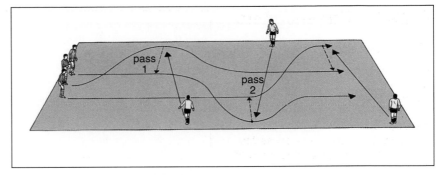

Fig 163 Creating space.

Counter-Attack

Fig 164 Patterns of counter-attack. Work in threes along a channel. Ball is kicked to the full-back.

Fig 165 He switches with the blind side wing after running back towards the kicker.

Fig 166 Blind side and open side wings to link up.

Counter-Attack (2)

Fig 167 Ball kicked to the open side wing.

Fig 168 A dummy switch with the full-back.

Fig 169 Switch with the blind side wing who now has the full-back as a passing option.

gives a switch to the blind-side wing going towards the open.

In a further development, five play against three in a 15 × 15m grid. The coach kicks the ball to five counter-attackers (two up level with the coach and three back). The midfield players run back to help counter-attack as the defenders come into the exercise. The defenders are arranged with two up and one back, so there are two lines of defence to beat.

Defence

Man-for-Man

Have two sets of tackle bags side by side about 2 metres apart, 5 metres between each set. Four players interlock their arms, approach the first set (Fig 172) and, on the signal, disconnect and tackle the correct bag in front of them. They then interlock arms again and sweep around on to the next set.

Progress to five against five, a scrum half on each side and three midfield defenders with a blind-side wing sweeping. (Fig 173). An attacking side pass goes to the end player, who is tackled by the

Counter-Attack (3)

Fig 170 Ball kicked to the blind side wing. A long pass to the full-back as a passing option.

Fig 171 He supports the full-back who has a passing option on the outside with the open side wing.

sweeper. A maul or ruck is simulated (Fig 174). The attackers go to the far side and the defenders do the same as the ball emerges for a second strike – three on three.

Drift Defence

Set up a line of tackle bags numbered one to six (Fig 175). The players go in threes from the same starting point. The coach shouts out a number. The first player has to tackle the nominated bag and his two partners have to tackle the next two bags outside it.

Now place four tackle bags midway between two groups of threequarters (Fig 176). The ball is passed from the scrum half to the attacking line who gets the ball to the end player. The defenders tackle the bags. The first defender stands opposite the first bag and drifts out to tackle the second bag, the second defender tackles the third bag, the third defender the fourth bag and the fourth defender tackles the ball carrier.

Now place four tackle bags 5 metres apart on the 5-metre line with cones opposite on the touch-line. The tacklers line up behind another cone. The first player tackles the first bag from the first cone, gets up and runs back to the cone opposite the bag he has just tackled. From here he will run at the next bag as a second tackler joins him and starts at the first cone. Both players hit their respective bags at the same time and a third player joins in. The tacklers approach the bags at an angle as if they were drifting.

Decision-Making

On the command, 1 and 2 go around a corner cone to attack a channel defended by 3 (Fig 178). The coach distributes the ball by passing to the near or far player or by rolling it into the channel. After the play, the players rotate positions: 3 goes to 1, 2 to 3 and 1 to 2.

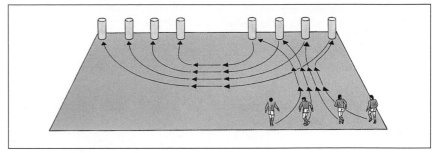

Fig 172 Defence: man-for-man.

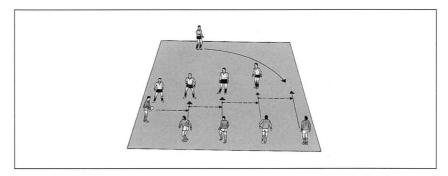

Fig 173 Defence progression (1).

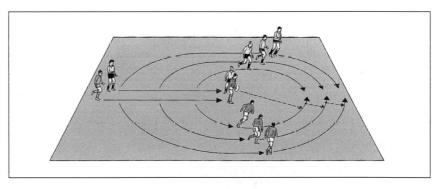

Fig 174 Man-for-man defence drill.

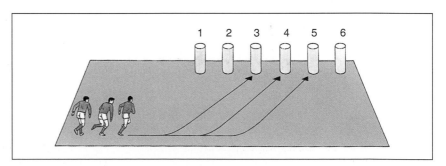

Fig 175 Drift defence drill. In this example bag 3 has been nominated.

Develop the drill with the threequarter line ready to attack from a lineout on the 22-metre line. The opposition is lined up across the goal-line and is numbered off. When the ball is in the scrum half's hands, the coach shouts out two numbers and the nominated defenders come out to defend. The attacking backs have to assess where the gaps and space are. Progress to calling out more defenders and mix up the defenders as the backs get used to where the gaps are from the numbers called out by the coach.

Now have an attacking group bunched together with a group of defenders opposite (Fig 179). On the signal, the defenders have each to choose a cone to run around before defending, and the attacking group attempts to score.

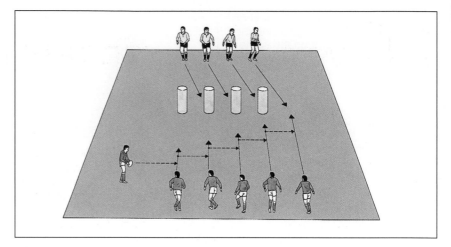

Fig 176 Drift defence drill – progression.

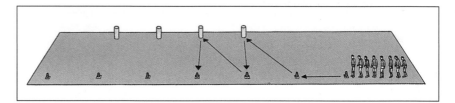

Fig 177 Drift defence drill – further progression.

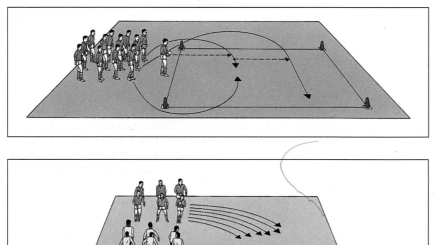

Fig 178 Decision making drill.

Fig 179 Decision making drill – progression.

CHAPTER 17

STANDARD PLOYS FOR THREEQUARTERS

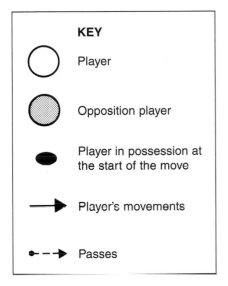

KEY

○ Player

◉ Opposition player

● Player in possession at the start of the move

•——▶ Player's movements

•--▶ Passes

Striking Close to the Forwards

Ploy 1

Field position: lineout.
Actions: fly half draws opposition open-side flanker, gives a pop pass to first centre on an inside diagonal run (Fig 180).
Passing options: inside to No.8 or outside to open-side flanker.

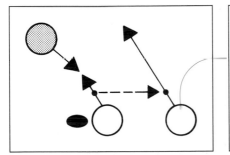

Fig 180 Striking close to the forwards, Ploy 1.

Ploy 2

Field position: lineout, scrum on left or right of midfield, second phase.
Actions: fly half makes a parallel run across midfield with the inside centre. The outside centre crosses behind the inside centre to take a switch pass from the fly half.
Passing options: inside to No.7 and 8; outside to fly half.

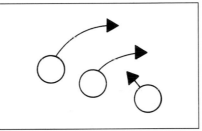

Fig 181 Striking close to the forwards, Ploy 2.

Ploy 3

Field position: lineout, scrums (maximum 25 metres from touch-line).
Actions: fly half to inside centre. Fly half dummy loop inside centre. Inside centre gives inside pass to blind-side wing on diagonal burst (Fig 182).
Passing options: outside to fly half, inside to back row.

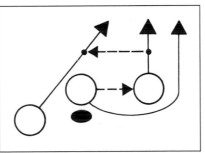

Fig 182 Striking close to the forwards, Ploy 3.

Striking in Midfield

Ploy 1

Field position: lineout, left or right.
Actions: fly half passes to and loops first centre. Receives return pass and passes to blind-side wing who passes to the full back. The second centre creates room by running wide (Fig 183).
Passing options: outside to second centre, inside to back row.

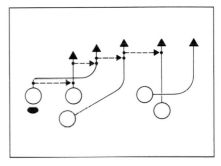

Fig 183 Striking in midfield, Ploy 1.

Ploy 2

Field position: lineout or scrum
Actions: fly half misses inside centre who loops outside the outside centre (Fig 184). Outside centre dummies a

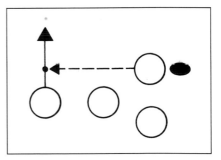

Fig 184 Striking in midfield, Ploy 2.

pass to him but gives the ball inside to the blind-side wing on a straight run (Fig 185).

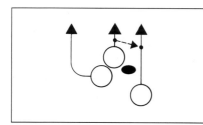

Fig 185 Striking in midfield, Ploy 2.

Passing options: outside to inside centre or inside to fly half.
Development: fly half misses inside centre who loops the outside centre. This is a dummy run and the second centre pops the ball to the full back on a straight run (Fig 186).

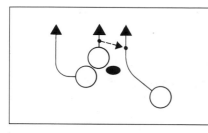

Fig 186 Striking in midfield, Ploy 2 – development.

Ploy 3

Field position: lineout or wide scrum (maximum 40 metres from touch).
Actions: fly half dummy switch with inside centre, switching with the blind-side wing on a diagonal run outside the inside centre (Fig 187).

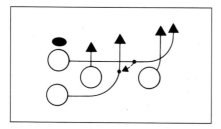

Fig 186 Striking in midfield, Ploy 3.

Passing options: outside to outside centre, inside to open-side flanker.

Ploy 4

Field position: lineout, scrum, second phase.
Actions: fly half to inside centre, diagonal run to dummy switch with outside centre giving pop pass to full back on straight run behind second centre (Fig 188).

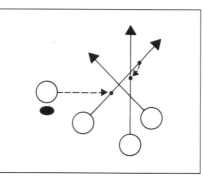

Fig 188 Striking in midfield, Ploy 4.

Passing options: outside to wing, inside to fly half.

Striking Wide

Ploy 1

Field position: lineout, scrum or second phase in 15-metre area.
Actions: fly half gives quick pass and receives a return pass on the run around. gives long pass to full back on wide run (Fig 189).

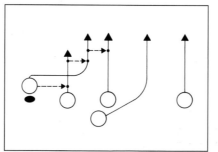

Fig 189 Striking wide, Ploy 1.

Passing options: outside to wing, inside to outside centre.

Ploy 2

Field position: lineout, scrum or second phase in 15-metre area.
Actions: fly half gives quick pass and receives a return pass on the run around. Outside centre drifts wide as the full back enters the line in his place on a dummy run. Fly half passes to the second centre (Fig 190).

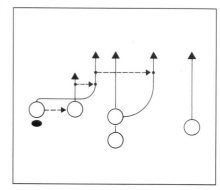

Fig 190 Striking wide, Ploy 2.

Ploy 3

Field position: lineout, scrum or second phase in 15-metre area.
Actions: fly half gives quick pass and receives a return pass on the run around. Outside centre drifts wide as the full back enters the line in his place and fly half pops the ball to the full back close (Fig 191).

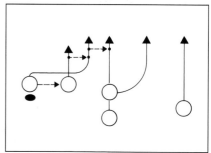

Fig 191 Striking wide, Ploy 3.

Fig 192 Striking wide: Ploy 2. Scrum half passes to fly half.

Fig 193 Fly half to inside centre as outside centre drifts wide.

Fig 194 Inside centre returns the pass to fly who is running around him. Full-back comes through the middle on a dummy run.

Fig 195 Full-back is missed out. Fly half passes to second run.

Fig 196 Three-quarters ploy – the playmaker is the player with the hooped socks, the fly half.

Fig 197 He passes to the inside centre.

Fig 198 The first centre passes back inside to him as he runs around.

Fig 199 The second centre drifts wide to allow the full-back to run on a straight line through the midfield.

Fig 200 The full-back has the passing option of the outside centre on his outside.

Ploy 4

Field position: lineout, scrum or second phase in 15-metre area.
Actions: fly half passes to inside centre and loops. At the same time, the outside centre loops the wing. Quick transfer to get the ball wide (Fig 201).
Options: exploit gaps or move the ball to space.

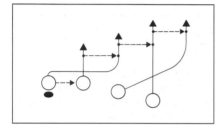

Fig 201 Striking wide, Ploy 4.

Ploy 5

Field position: lineout, left or right.
Actions: fly half to inside centre to outside centre. Outside centre switches with full back and full back switches with blind-side wing (Fig 202).
Passing options: outside to open-side wing, inside to centres in support.

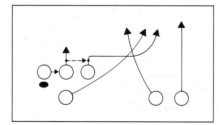

Fig 202 Striking wide, Ploy 5.

Midfield Scrums

A midfield scrum is a prime attacking position because the defence will be spread across the width of the field. There are also more options for the attacking side. The back three are further apart and have more to think about.

It is important for the attacking side to cross the gain-line quickly to outflank the back row, so any moves chosen should not take place too deep behind the scrum.

Ploy 1

Field position: midfield scrum.
Channel: wide.
Actions: the left side is packed with the attacking midfield and left wing to clear space on the right for the full back to run into and receive a pass directly from the scrum half (Fig 203). The right wing stands wide to take his opposite number wide thus also creating space for the full back. The full back should receive a flat pass to cross the gain-line quickly.
Passing options: outside to wing, inside to back row.
Comments: this move creates a problem for the defence. The defending full back cannot stand up in the space because it leaves a huge area behind him and no one

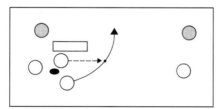

Fig 203 Midfield scrums, Ploy 1.

able to cover a kick into it. The back row and fly half cannot get across quickly enough.

Ploy 2

Field position: midfield scrum.
Channel: wide.
Actions: scrum half passes directly to the centre who passes to the looping fly half (Fig 204). The centre must be running on to the pass and must distribute the ball before being tackled by his opposite centre.
Passing options: outside to wing, inside to back row.

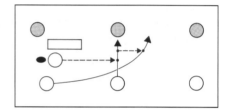

Fig 204 Midfield scrums, Ploy 2.

Practising Threequarters' Moves

Drill 1 (Fig 205)

Scrum half starts in Position 1 with a ball. He passes to Group A, who pass the ball along to the end player,

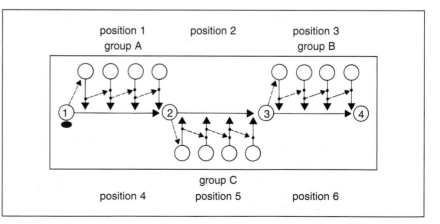

Fig 205 Three-quarters Drill 1.

who places it at Position 2. The scrum half passes from this position to Group C who run forwards and the end player places the ball at position 3 for the scrum half to pass to Group B. The end player of this group places the ball at 4.

Group A continue their run from Position 1 to the opposite side of the grid to Position 4. They then run to Position 6 to receive a pass from the scrum half when he gets to Position 4. Group A then cross the grid and run on to Position 1 again.

Group C cross the grid to Position 2 and return to Position 5 again when the scrum half passes from position 3 on his return run.

Group B run to Position 6 and continue on to Position 4. When the scrum half passes to them from Position 2, the Group crosses to Position 1 and continues on to Position 3 again.

Drill 2

In a shuttle relay, each group of four or five players takes it in turn to cross the grid. One ball only is needed.

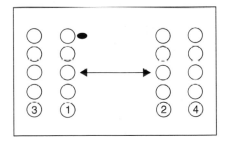

Fig 206 Three-quarters Drill 2.

Drill 3

Cones are placed in an 'L' shape, spaced about 2 or 3 metres apart and a player is stationed at each cone. The ball is passed through every pair of hands from 1 to 4. These players stand still at their stations. Player 4 becomes a scrum half and passes the ball to 5, the outside half. The moves are then

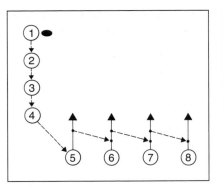

Fig 207 Three-quarters Drill 3.

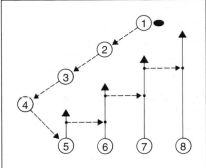

Fig 208 Three-quarters Drill 3 – changing the angles.

performed by Players 5, 6, 7, and 8 (Fig 207)

All players rotate (8 to 1, 1 to 2, 2 to 3 and so on). Players 1 to 4 can be placed at different angles so that Players 5 to 8 have targets in front of them (Fig 208). Players 1 to 4 can become active opposition once 5 has got the ball. The following moves are to be practised with these drills:

- Player 1 misses 2 and passes to 3 (Fig 209(a)). Player 3 runs back in and switches with 2 going out. Player 2 out to 4 (Fig 209(b)).
- Player 1 passes to 3 who passes to 4 (Fig 210(a)). Player 4 runs back in and does an outward switch with 3. Player 2 loops to end to receive a pass from 3 (Fig 210(b)).
- Player 1 passes to 3. Players 1

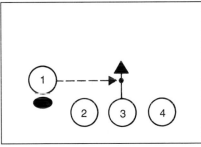

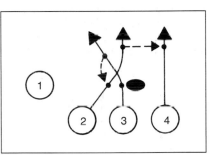

Fig 209(a)–209(b)   Moves to practise with three-quarters drills (1).

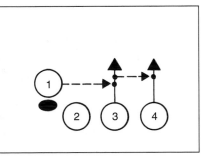

Fig 210(a)–210(b)   Moves to practise with three-quarters drills (2).

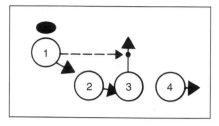

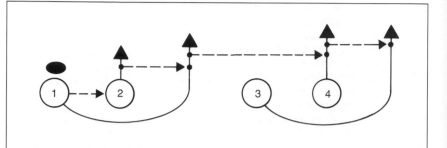

Fig 212 Player 2 loops to end to receive a pass from 3.

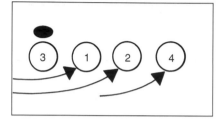

Fig 211 Moves to practise with three-quarters drills (3).

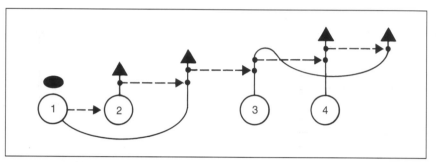

Fig 213 Player 3 loops 4 to receive a pass.

and 2 loop 3. Player 1 takes the inside track so they both run the same distance (Fig 211).

• Player 1 passes to 2. Player 1 loops 2 to receive a return pass. Player 2 misses 3 to pass to 4 changing angle and coming in close. 3 loops 4 to receive a pass (Fig 212).

• Player 1 passes to 2 and loops for a return pass. Player 1 passes to 3 who passes to 4 and loops 4 for a return pass (Fig 213).

• Player 1 passes to 2. Players 2 and 3 switch. Player 3 passes to 4 supported by 2 who continued his run to the end of the line (Fig 214).

• Player 1 dummy switches with 2 and switches with 3. Player 3 passes to 4 coming in close. Player 1 continues his run to the end and receives a pass from 4 (Fig 215).

Variations

• First player passes and loops to the end (Fig 216).
• First and second player pass and loop to the end – becomes: 3, 4, 1, 2.
• First player passes and loops to the end as the end man – the ball

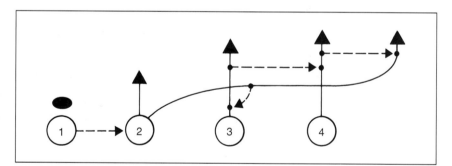

Fig 214 Players 2 and 3 switch and 3 passes to 4.

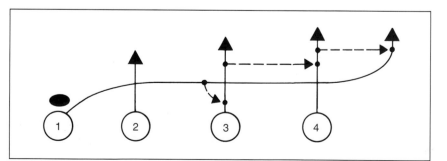

Fig 215 Player 1 dummy switches with 2 and switches with 3.

carrier – does an outward switch with his inside man – becomes: 2, 4, 3, 1.

• Second player misses out the third and passes to the fourth player. The player missed out loops to the end – becomes: 1, 2, 4, 3.

• First player passes and loops to the end. second player misses out the third and passes to the fourth. The player missed out loops to the end – becomes: 2, 4, 3, 1.

• Two end players do a switch – becomes: 1, 2, 4, 3.

• Player 1 to 2 to 3. Player 2 loops 3 or passes back inside for the run-around. Two end players must delay their run, hang back and then run.

• Player 1 to 2 who passes back inside to 1 on a run-around. Player 3 on a dummy run and is missed out. The ball is passed straight to 4 (Fig 217).

• Player 1 to 2 who passes inside to 1 on a run around. Player 1 switches with 3 who passes to 4. Player 1 continues the run to the end to receive a pass from 4 (Fig 218).

• Player 1 misses 2. Player 3 switches with 4 and 4 switches with 2 (Fig 219).

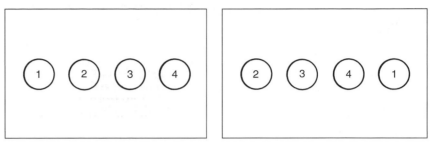

Fig 216 First player passes and loops to the end.

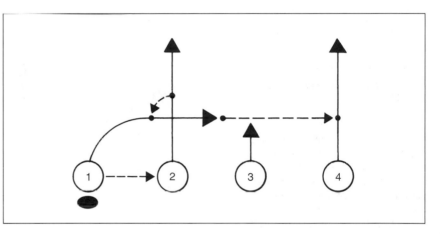

Fig 217 Player 1 passes to 2, who passes back. Player 3 is missed out.

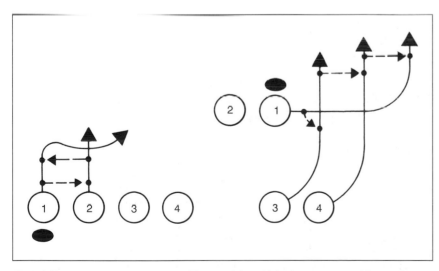

Fig 218 Players 1 and 2 pass to each other. Then 1 switches with 3, who passes to 4, while 1 continues his run to the end.

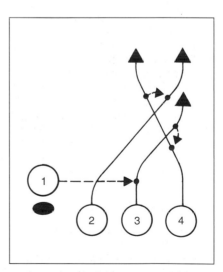

Fig 219 Player 3 switches with 4 and 4 switches with 2.

CHAPTER 18

COUNTER-ATTACK FROM KICK RECEIPT

The Role of the Full Back

With a positive attitude of mind and self-confidence in his own ability, a full back can launch counter-attacks from deep opposition kicks, long 22 drop-outs or long kicks at goal.

Sometimes, the full back will have to field a high ball, at other times he will have to retrieve a ball rolling on the ground either in front or behind him. Sometimes he will be faced by a broken field, at other times by a well-organized chase. The decision whether to run, kick or pass will have to be taken. He must avoid being caught in possession behind his support. He will operate with his wings who are deeper than the midfield and can usually get back to help out. There will have to be communication between the three and some form of organization or movement pattern in place.

The full back concentrates on the ball. He lacks the peripheral vision of the support player and it is the support player who helps him take the decision to counter. However, if the receiver catches the ball cleanly and running at full speed, he does not need someone else to decide whether or not he should counter-attack.

There are a number of key factors in a successful counter: the support player helps the fielder of the ball in decision-making; the counter-attack is made only if the kick is poor and the ball is immediately available; the ball is brought forward with pace; the player dummies to strength by running towards the congested areas, then taking the ball into space; the ball is played before contact.

Counter-Attack from a Turn-Over Ball

Possession from a turn-over is the best opportunity to launch an attack, whilst the opposition's mind-set is still in attack mode. The key principles are to move the ball away from the turn-over point; scan the defence and either attack a mismatch or get ball to players in space (scan, talk, react). A mismatch occurs where a threequarter's immediate defender is a forward. If the ball is moved quickly away from the breakdown, either with two quick passes or a miss pass from the fly half, the attack will be launched into space.

Exercises for Directing and Initiating Counter-Attack from Kick Receipt

Drill 1

Player A1 throws ball to B1 and chases to oppose. Player B1 runs back at A1 and works with C1 to beat him with a switch or offload early if under pressure (high ball). The support is to be the 'eyes' of the ball retriever and communicate when to pass. Both should bring the ball forwards quickly; fix the chaser. Players are to rotate – A joins queue B and so on (Fig 220).

Drill 2

• Players in threes with one ball run over 15m going through counter-attack patterns.
• Player 1 passes and loops 2.
• Player 3 dummy switches with 2 and switches with 1.
• Players 1 passes to 2. Player 2 switches with 1 and 1 passes to 3.
• Player 2 switches with 3; 3 switches with 1 and 1 passes to 2.

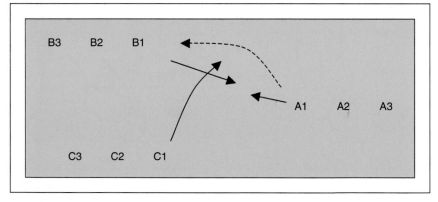

Fig 220 Exercises for Directing and Initiating Counter-Attack from Kick Receipt Drill 1.

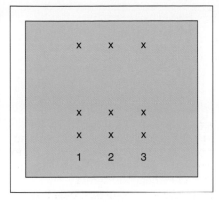

Fig 221 Exercises for Directing and Initiating Counter-Attack from Kick Receipt Drill 2.

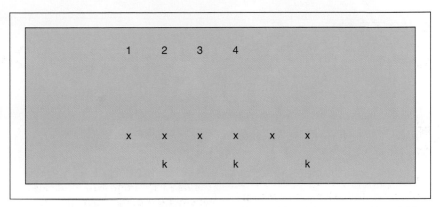

Fig 222 Exercises for Counter-Attack from a Turn-Over Ball Drill 2.

Counter-Attack Game

One team A stands underneath the goal-posts; the opposition B stands in the field of play covering as much ground as they are able. One player from Team A kicks and Team B retrieves the ball and aims to bring the ball back to score anywhere on the goal-line. Every player in his side has to receive and give a pass. Team A tries to stop them by sending initially one defender to chase the kick. If he touches a ball carrier, he has won the contest and the sides swap over. If the attacking side scores, the kicking team sends up two defenders then, if they fail, three defenders, and so on, until they are successful in catching the attacking side in possession of the ball. Gradually, a kicking strategy, a chasing strategy and the principles of counter-attack will emerge.

Exercises for Counter-Attack from a Turn-Over Ball

Drill 1

A group of three players pass a ball as they move towards five defenders. When they are close to the defenders, the ball carrier is to roll the ball to them. They then defend as the five try to outflank or penetrate as appropriate against the three.

Drill 2

Two of the initial defending side are on their knees. The attacking side takes the tackle. The player on the inside shoulder of the tackler steps over to win the ball and plays it away. The new attack tries to get behind the new defence.

Player 2, 3 or 4 takes the ball up into a player on his knees for the turn-over counter-attack to start.

PART 7

PHYSICAL AND MENTAL FITNESS

LIFESTYLE

Achieving in rugby depends on having the right attitude. Attitude is reflected in a determined approach to training. Lifestyle should not interfere with but, rather, complement a training programme.

Sleep

Sleep is the means by which humans recuperate physically, mentally and psychologically. Lack of sleep produces fatigue, slower reflexes and loss of stamina. What constitutes the proper amount of sleep will vary from individual to individual. On average, a person needs about eight hours per night. The correct amount for each invidual, however, is whatever that person needs in order to wake up in the morning feeling energetic. Each individual should ascertain his own needs and get the minimum amount of sleep consistently.

Rest

The body needs to replenish its energy stores the day before a match, and players should not train hard, or indulge in physical activity for long periods. Hot baths or saunas on the day before a game are exhausting and to be avoided. This is an opportunity to relax and enjoy a diversion from the daily routine.

Fluid Balance

Be fully hydrated before taking exercise. Thirst is a poor indicator of the need to take fluid, as, by the time a player feels thirsty, it is already too late. Drink water during training sessions. After exercise, start the rehydration process immediately, with water or commercial drinks containing additional carbohydrate.

Alcohol

The heavy use of alcohol is harmful and excessive intake will produce overweight players. Alcohol hangover decreases a player's stamina performance and alcohol should therefore not be consumed within 48 hours of the start of a game.

If alcohol has been taken up to 12 hours before an injury, the temporary heart stimulation and dilation of blood vessels can increase bleeding and add to the severity of the injury.

Before drinking alcohol after a game, first rehydrate with glucose and electrolyte-containing drinks. Two or three litres of fluid after a game will also help to stave off the dehydration that the alcohol may produce. Alcohol has a diuretic effect on the kidneys, in other words, it makes you pass larger quantities of urine, causing greater fluid losses.

Tobacco

Smoking harms the body's oxygen system and reduces a player's endurance ability. Nicotine and carbon monoxide make the heart beat faster than usual at a given intensity of exercise. Carbon monoxide also combines with the haemoglobin by which oxygen is carried in the blood. Less oxygen is transported and what is carried is less easily released to the muscle tissues.

Diet

Before and After Exercise

High-carbohydrate diets optimize performance. Complex carbohydrates that are high in fibre, protein, vitamins and minerals are wholegrain cereal products, fresh or dried fruit, vegetables, rice, bread, beans, potatoes, and lentils. However, for the correct intake of recommended carbohydrates a large amount of this food must be consumed. Avoid large meals. Smaller, more frequent high-carbohydrate meals are easier on the entire digestive system. Simple carbohydrates, such as confectionary and junk foods, have the same amount of carbohydrate intake in less bulk, but these foods are lacking in many nutrients and high in fat and sugar.

Pre-Match

In the days leading up to a match, you should make gradual increases in your carbohydrate intake. Eat a light meal the night before the match. On the day of the match, eat a breakfast consisting mainly of carbohydrates three to four hours before kick-off, to give it time to be properly digested. Toast with marmalade or honey is a good choice.

After Exercise

Start the refuelling process immediately after a match. The replenishment of muscle glycogen after exercise is a major factor in the recovery process. The rate of muscle glycogen resynthesis is faster in the two hours after exercise than at any other time. You should eat carbohydrates at this time.

CHAPTER 20

PERSONAL TRAINING

Components of Fitness

Simply, the components of fitness for rugby are stamina, speed, strength and suppleness. A fit player thinks and reacts more quickly, is less prone to injury, and is less likely to miss tackles and more likely to make a break and score. Good results will come from a conscientious input of energy and effort, and a degree of sacrifice.

Positional Requirements

Fitness programmes should be tailored to positional needs. Different positions have different requirements, for example, locks and props need to run at a constant speed and therefore require high aerobic (stamina/endurance) fitness. Back-row players, half-backs and hookers require equal amounts of aerobic and anaerobic (high-intensity/speed) fitness. The rest of the threequarters need basic aerobic fitness with a high anaerobic intensity component (speed and speed endurance).

Aerobic Endurance (Stamina)

In order to have an effect, aerobic training does not have to be at maximum level. A rough guide to training intensity can be found by subtracting a player's age from 220 to give an approximate maximal training pulse rate (count your pulse over 6 seconds and multiply by 10). Aerobic training means that the oxygen taken in is sufficient for the energy needs of the activity. The efficiency of heart, lungs, blood vessels and muscles to use and transport the oxygen to the working muscles is vital. The minimal duration is 20 minutes for continuous activity (running, swimming, rowing or cycling). For interval training, the minimal volume is 15 minutes.

Examples

Continuous Activity
•   3 miles of continuous running for 20 minutes with a 6-minute jog/walk recovery.
•   4 miles of continuous running for 28 minutes with an 8-minute jog/walk recovery.
•   5 miles in 35–40 minutes.

Interval Training
•   800 metres in 3 minutes, 6 repetitions, 3 minutes jog recovery between each run.
•   600 metres in 2 minutes, 8 repetitions, 2 minutes jog recovery between each run.
•   Long interval session: run for 3 minutes, faster than continuous running speed. Rest for 3 minutes. Do this 6 times. Try to reach the same mark or go further on each run.

Anaerobic Endurance (Speed and Speed Endurance)

Speed is the ability to move quickly and effectively. It depends on reaction time, speed of muscle contraction, strength and technique. To develop speed, do reaction drills, acceleration sprints, long sprints, agility sprints, technique training, incline running and weight-training.

The work periods should last no longer than 40 seconds. The volume of work should be between 10 and 20 minutes. Each exercise should be performed at maximum. To maintain the quality of work, rests must be adequate. A 1:6 ratio of work to rest should be followed between repetitions with approximately 10 minutes of active rest (for example, jogging to get rid of lactic waste) between sets.

Examples

•   50 metres in 7 seconds, 6 repetitions, 2 sets, 40 seconds rest between reps and 10 minutes between sets.
•   Running drills over 100 metres (for example, 33m with controlled use of arms, 33m at coasting speed, 33m fast legs). Walk to recover (2 minutes). 2 sets of 6 reps. 5 minutes between sets.
•   For speed endurance do shuttle runs of 10m, 20m, 40m, 60m, 40m, 20m, 10m.

Strength/Power

Strength refers to the ability of the muscles to exert force. It is the most important component of physical fitness because it contributes to endurance, agility and speed.

Strength is developed by performing any exercise that involves applying heavier than usual resistance. Alternatives to weight-training include sit-ups, press-ups, pull-ups, leg-raising and double knee jumps. Choose exercises which develop the chest and thigh regions particularly.

Strength is a necessary pre-requisite for increased power and is best gained by using heavy weights and low repetitions (4–6). The development of power is best achieved by using light weights with 3 sets of 10 reps, with the work part of the exercise being done at maximum speed and the recovery part slowly.

Plyometrics

Plyometric work increases leg power for jumping and acceleration. A plyometric session can be 3 sets of 6 reps. Allow 5 minutes rest between sets. Bounce from a box, up to 45cm (18in) high. Think of the floor as red hot and make an instant response by sprinting away for 5-10 metres or bouncing on to another box. Rebound and do not sink. As soon as the knees bend, jump.

KEY POINTS

These are important points to avoid injury during plyometric work:
• Wear proper footwear with non-slip sole, good ankle and arch support
• Work on a firm but giving training surface, warm up and stretch adequately
• Practise proper landing technique, aligning the ankle, knee and hip joints; all three joints should absorb the shock

Suppleness and Flexibility

Flexibility is very important as an aid to performance and also in preventing injury. Never stretch cold muscles. Do a slow jog for about 5 minutes and then do stretching exercises. Stretch to the beginning of tension, and hold for 20–30 seconds. Avoid bouncing.

Flexibility exercises are similar to

stretching exercise, but the tension is increased and the position is held at a comfortable level for 30–40 seconds. Improvement in these exercises allows a greater range of movement. Do these for 10 minutes at the end of a training session, particularly after weight-training.

Warm-Up and Warm-Down

A warm-up prepares the body for exercise. The risk of injury is less likely and you feel better and more able to cope with explosive exercise.

A warm-down period is equally important after all sessions and games. Gentle exercise helps the muscles get rid of waste products, thus reducing muscle soreness the next day.

Planning Your Programme

The year can be divided into various phases of training: off-season training or the recuperation phase (about four weeks); pre-season training (about eight weeks); and peak-season training or the competition phase, which lasts through the season, with varying periods of intensity.

Off-Season Phase

This period should be fun and involve active rest to avoid weight gain. It should include some muscular fitness and aerobic fitness training. It is also a period of reflection and goal-setting.

Pre-Season Phase

This phase begins about eight weeks before the start of the rugby season. It is a general preparatory phase and should include the following:

Fig 223 Chevvy Pennycook and James Phillips (Bristol Rugby) sprint training.

- muscular fitness training to develop the strength base. Three training sessions a week are enough to gain muscular fitness;
- aerobic fitness training such as long continuous running, fartlek training, easy-paced interval training and circuit work. If the session is of low intensity, this could be carried out on the same day as a weight training session;
- muscular endurance training. Pre-season training should include a variety of speed and endurance training sessions;
- as the season approaches, players will need to work more often on individual skills, and unit, team and tactical training. Power and speed training become more urgent. High-intensity training should be planned to build up to the competitive phase;
- anaerobic fitness is critical; around six weeks of high-intensity anaerobic workouts two to three times per week should be sufficient.

Peak-Season Training (Competitive Phase)

Rugby has a long competitive season and players are effectively required to 'peak' every week throughout that season. However, by looking at the season as a whole and considering the relative strength of the opposition, and identifying 'hot' and 'cool' periods, it is possible to plan training so that players peak at really important times.

Technical and tactical work continues but the conditioning can be incorporated into this training by considering the intensity and length of each session. Use competitive drills and activities that simulate typical competitive conditions.

As the height of the competitive season approaches, muscular and energy fitness training typically culminates in an emphasis on quality and speed. Players should concentrate on high-speed and low-resistance movements and sprints.

CHAPTER 21

TREATMENT OF INJURIES

Common Injuries

Fractures and dislocations need immediate medical treatment. Consideration must also be given to the following.

Sprains

Sprains are caused when the ligaments, which bind opposing bony surfaces together, are forced beyond their normal range, leading to stretching or tearing and displaced joint surfaces.

Strains

A strain is an overstretching of a muscle or tendon.

Ruptured Blood Vessels

These are impact injuries.

Treatment

The purpose of treatment is first to prevent the blood formation in large mass, and second to prevent any adhesions (bumps) that delay normal movement.

'RICE'

In all forms of exercise, blood circulation increases (the pulse quickens), thus when an injury occurs, bleeding into the tissue cavities is much quicker, causing swelling and pain. The larger the muscle, the more blood it contains. To keep bleeding to the minimum or slow it down in the injured area, remember the all-important acronym 'RICE' as immediate treatment:

- Rest: relax the injured part.
- Ice: apply a cold compress of ice over the injured area. Bucket and sponge is the quickest and cheapest way of applying cold on the field of play but, because of the risk from infection, do not apply on open wounds and add antiseptic to the water. Ice packs, icy water, ice cube massage, even a bag of frozen peas may all be used.
- Compression: compression is applied to the injured area, using cotton wool, a sponge, or an elasticized non-adhesive bandage.
- Elevation: elevate the area. Blood flows slower uphill.

> **KIT CHECK**
>
> All players should undergo a course of tetanus injections.

Continue this treatment as soon as possible after the injury has been sustained and for as long as practicable, for no less than 48 hours. Remember, however, that the first hour of treatment is the most important.

Other Important Points

Do not apply heat because heat increases circulation, causing further swelling and pain. Keep shower time

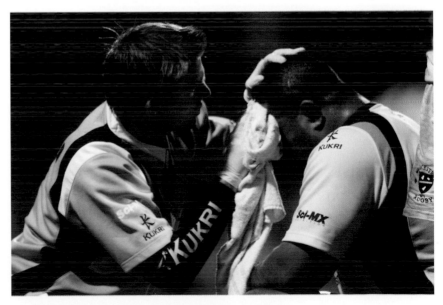

Fig 224 Tevita Taumoepeau of Worcester warriors receiving treatment.

to a minimum. Never sit in a hot bath. Never use heat lamps within 48 hours of an injury. Standing on an injured lower limb for a long time can cause further pain.

Alcohol should not be taken within 12 hours of injury, particularly in the case of severe muscle injuries. After 48 hours start gentle, active, unrestrictive exercise, depending on the severity of the injury.

Physiotherapy consists of various methods of stimulation of the injured area, particularly deep-seated injuries, which are otherwise difficult to treat quickly. It should help to restore normal movement. After physiotherapy has been stopped, the player should continue with

---

KIT CHECK

Do not forget a pre-match check of first aid equipment and supplies. Know where the phone is in case of a need to ring the emergency services. A stretcher, splints, bandages and ice should be available.

---

resistance and stretching exercises designed to increase the strength and flexibility in the affected area.

Strapping techniques should always be supplementary, and not replace the joint protection afforded by exercises to strengthen appropriate muscles.

Head Injuries

Guidelines have been drawn up by the International RugbyBoard to help deal with players who have had a head injury or concussion. Players who have suffered concussion or loss of consciousness should not train or play rugby for at least three weeks, and then only after they have been cleared to do so by a doctor. A second head injury before there has been full recovery from the first may have serious consequences.

Concussion occurs when the brain is injured following a blow to the head or face. The signs and symptoms of concussion include loss of consciousness; loss of memory; confusion and disorientation; double or blurred vision; giddiness or

unsteadiness; vomiting; headache. Being unaware of what happened for even a few moments at the time of the injury is the most consistent sign that the player is concussed.

A player exhibiting any of these symptoms should stop training or playing, and be referred for medical attention. The player must be taken immediately to hospital if there is any reason for concern or if the player has been unconscious for any length of time.

It is important to look after concussed players or players who have been unconscious, as they are unable to look after themselves properly or take rational decisions. No player should be left alone, given alcohol or allowed to drive a vehicle until their head injury or concussion has been medically assessed. Potentially serious complications can develop up to 24 hours after an apparently minor head injury. The following symptoms may develop due to a deteriorating head injury: headache which persists; drowsiness leading to unconsciousness; irritability; confusion and loss of concentration; vomiting; convulsions.

GLOSSARY

Alignment   The shape of the threequarter line, either in attack or defence.

Backs or threequarters   The players numbered 9 to 15 outside the forwards.

Binding   A player using his whole arm to hold on to a team-mate, for example, in the scrum.

Blind-side   Originally the blind-side of the referee, the far side of the scrum or ruck and maul from which the referee is standing. Now the term generally refers to the narrow corridor between the touch-line and the scrum, ruck and maul rather than the open-side.

Cross-binding   When a ball carrier goes into contact with a defender, cross-binding refers to the two immediate support players, who do not bind on the ball carrier but bind on each other. This leaves the ball carrier free to go to ground when he chooses without pulling the other two players with him.

Drop-goal   Three points can be scored if a player takes a snap drop-kick at goal during a passage of play and the ball goes over the cross-bar and between the uprights.

Drop-kick   The drop-kick restarts the game at 22-metre drop-outs and from the half-way line after a score. The ball must first touch the ground before the kick is launched.

Fixing (a defender)   The ball carrier's intention is to draw a defender to him or fix him to the spot, so he can release the ball at the right time. The defender will then be unable to defend against the new ball carrier.

Flanker   There are two flankers numbered 6 and 7. They bind on to the locks, on the flanks of the scrum. They are used to defend against players attacking close to the scrum. The blind-side flanker (6) covers the narrow channel near the scrum and the open-side flanker (7) covers the larger spaces on the other side of the scrum.

Forwards   The players numbered 1 to 8 who form the scrum and the lineout.

Full back   The No.15, the threequarter who stands at the back of the line to field any kicks over the threequarter line and to sweep behind the line to tackle any player who breaks through or outflanks it. The last line of defence.

Gain-line   An imaginary line across the pitch through the centre of the scrum, lineout and ruck and maul. If the attacking side crosses it with the ball, they are gaining ground and going forwards.

Half-backs   The scrum half (9) and fly half (10).

Half-break   This occurs when a player with the ball gets tackled and cannot make a clean break through the defence. He just gets behind the defender to pass the ball to a support player who does pierce the line.

Hand-off   When a player has the ball, he may prevent a defender tackling him by handing him off. This must not be in a dangerous way and is generally done with open palm and bent arm straightening and pushing away the would-be tackler.

Hang time   The amount of time the ball is in the air after being kicked.

Hooker   The No.2 in the forwards. He hooks the ball back in the scrum with his feet and is supported on either side by the props Nos.1 and 3. He generally throws in the ball at the lineouts.

Infield   The area in the field of play and away from the touch-lines.

Inside centre   The No. 12, the first centre, tends to be big and strong because he has to do a lot of tackling, and he takes the ball into the heart of the opposing threequarter line to disrupt it.

Knock-on   Occurs when the ball first touches the hand or arm of a player and is propelled forwards towards his opponent's dead-ball line and hits the ground.

Lineout   A throw-in occurs after the ball has gone into touch. The ball is thrown into the lineout, down the middle of two opposing lines of players.

Locks   The lock forwards are numbered 4 and 5 and originally named to lock the scrum and prevent it being pushed backwards.

Loop   After making a pass, a player can support the ball carrier by looping him. This means that he runs around the ball carrier to his outside so that he can receive a return pass.

Loose-head prop   No.1, the outside prop in the scrum, who holds up the hooker.

Midfielders   The fly half and two centres. They are the middle link between the forwards and the outside players, the wings and full back.

Midi Rugby   Rugby is introduced gradually to young people and the Rugby Football Union has devised a continuum whereby the laws change at different age groups. Midi Rugby refers to the Under-12 age group, the stage between the Minis and the full fifteen-a-side game. The game is played by twelve players (five forwards and seven backs) across the field from goal-line to touch-line. The scrum has three front rows and two locks. Hand-offs are forbidden.

Mini Rugby   Played by age groups from Under 9 to Under 11, with tackling, scrummaging and lineouts being gradually introduced. Each team has nine a side (three forwards and six backs).

Miss pass   If a ball carrier has two players to whom he is able to pass on his outside, and he passes to the one further away, he has missed a player out and given a miss pass.

Open-side   The large channel, the wide open spaces left when the forwards are grouped together at scrums and rucks and mauls. The open-side flanker is responsible for operating in this space, so he must be very quick, agile and tireless.

Outside centre   There are two centres, Nos.12 and 13. The outside centre, the second centre (13), tends to be quick and elusive and operates in more space than the first centre, who is closer to the forwards.

Pad holder   In training, a player who holds a contact shield or pad; these are now widely used in practice to prevent injury in contact.

Passing line   The imaginary line along which the ball travels from scrum half to wing.

Platform   The launching point for an attack is usually provided by the forwards at scrum, lineout, and ruck and maul. These must be solid and moving forwards if they are to be an effective platform.

Pop pass   A short, very soft pass using hands and wrists with very little arm movement.

Rip   The action of aggressively wrestling the ball from an opponent.

Scrum   A set piece that can take place only in the field of play and is formed by players from each team binding together so that the heads of the front rows are interlocked. A tunnel is created and the scrum half puts the ball in down the middle of the tunnel.

Scrum half   The No.9, originally so named because he is half-way back between the forwards (the scrum) and the backs. He is the link between both units, the ball providers (the forwards) and the ball users (the threequarters or backs).

Smother tackle   An all-embracing tackle around the upper body, which smothers the ball and prevents the ball carrier getting the ball away.

Spilled ball   When a ball carrier gets tackled so aggressively that he loses control of the ball and drops it.

Strike runner   The player who intends to break through the defence. The aim is to get the ball to him, with other players being a distraction to the defenders.

Sweeper   A player who is looking to clean up any ball that has been dropped or any ball that the ball carrier needs help in controlling.

Tackle line   An imaginary line where the contact between the two teams takes place. It is usually where the two sets of threequarters collide. If the defenders and attackers are running at the same speed, this line is equidistant from their starting positions.

Threequarters   Term that originally applied to the centres and wings who were threequarters of the way back between the forwards and the full back. Now the term applies to all the backs numbered from 9 to 15.

Tight-head prop   The (inside) prop, No.3, in the scrum who holds up the hooker.

Touch-line   The boundary on either side of the playing area. The touch-lines must not be more than 69 metres apart.

Upfield   The area far away from each team's own goal-line, up the field.

FURTHER READING

Black, Alan, *How to Coach Rugby Football* (Willow Books, 1990)

Greenwood, Jim, *Think Rugby* (A & C Black, 1986)

Johnson, P., *Rugby for Threequarters* with Richard Hill (A & C Black, 1993)

Johnson, P., *Rugby Lesson Plans for Threequarters* with Jonathan Webb (A & C Black, 1994)

Rugby Union *Laws of the Game* (IRB)

INDEX